Muslims: Why the Violence

VOLUME 2

STUDIES IN CHRISTIAN-MUSLIM RELATIONS

OTHER BOOKS WRITTEN OR EDITED BY DR. JAN H. BOER

The Prophet Moses for Today

Abraham Kuyper: You Can Do Greater Things than Christ (trans / ed.)

Science Without Faith Is Dead
(Under same cover with above)

Wholistic Health Care (Co-editor: Dr. Dennis Ityavyar)

Vol. 1: Medical and Religious Dimensions

Vol. 2: Social and Political Dimensions

Wholistic Health Care Of, For and By the People

Caught in the Middle: Christians in Transnational Corporations

The Church and the External Debt (edited)

Missions: Heralds of Capitalism or Christ?

Missionary Messengers of Liberation in a Colonial Context

For more details, see his Web site:

www.SocialTheology.com

NIGERIA'S DECADES OF BLOOD

JAN H. BOER

Essence
PUBLISHING

Belleville, Ontario, Canada

Muslims: Why the Violence?

National Library of Canada Cataloguing in Publication

Boer, Jan Harm

Muslims : why the violence? / Jan H. Boer.

(Studies in Christian-Muslim relations ; v. 2)

Cover title.

Includes bibliographical references and index.

ISBN 1-55306-719-3.--ISBN 1-55306-721-5 (LSI ed.)

1. Violence--Religious aspects--Islam. 2. Violence--Nigeria--History--20th century. 3. Islam--Nigeria. 4. Islam--Relations--Christianity. 5. Christianity and other religions--Islam. I. Title. II. Series: Boer, Jan Harm . Studies in Christian-Muslim relations ; v. 2.

BP64.N49B64 2004 297'.09669 C2004-900321-6

For more information please contact:

Dr. Jan H. Boer at Boerjf@hotmail.com

Web site: www.SocialTheology.com

Essence Publishing

20 Hanna Court, Belleville, Ontario, Canada K8P 5J2.

Phone: 1-800-238-6376 • Fax: (613) 962-3055.

E-mail: publishing@essencegroup.com

Internet: www.essencegroup.com

Nigerian Edition © 2004 by:

Stream Christian Publishers

6, Noad Ave. (Behind Central Bank)

P.O. Box 13377, Jos, Plateau State

Tel.: 73-458541 • Mobile: 803-7181354

E-mail: chrisb@skannet.com

I dedicate this volume to the Nigerians who have contributed significantly to my development and ministry in Nigeria.

Evangelist Ifraimu Nyajo
Rev. Dr. David G. Angye
Alhaji Muhammad Nyajo
Rev. Akila W. Machunga
Rev. Dr. Prof. Ishaya Audu
Hon. Justice Haruna Dandaura
Late Rev. Dr. Jabanni Mambula
Late Ambassador J. Tanko Yusuf
Elder James Kpanto
Bishop Dr. A. E. Adegbola

These fathers and brothers of mine may not necessarily agree with all the opinions expressed in these pages, but I do thank them for the role they have played in my formation, for the hand of fellowship they have extended to me—and for correcting me! Allah ya ba da lada! Amin.

TABLE OF CONTENTS

ABBREVIATIONS

ABU	Ahmadu Bello University
CAN	Christian Association of Nigeria
CC	*Christian Courier* (Canadian bi-weekly)
CRC	Christian Reformed Church
GTFK	*Gaskiya Ta Fi Kwabo* (Hausa newspaper)
ICS	Institute for Church and Society
IMF	International Monetary Fund
IRK	Islamic Religious Knowledge
JNI	Jama'atul Nasril Islam
MSS	Muslim Students Society
NACOMYO	National Council of Muslim Youth Organisations
NC	*National Concord*
NEPA	Nigerian Electrical Power Authority
NEPU	Northern Element Progressive Union
NIPSS	National Institute for Policy and Strategic Studies
NIREC	Nigeria Inter-Religious Council
NN	*New Nigerian*
NPC	Northern People's Congress
NPN	National Party of Nigeria
NS	*Nigeria Standard*
NTA	Nigerian Television Authority
NYSC	National Youth Service Corps

OIC	Organisation of Islamic Conference
OPEC	Organization of Petroleum Exporting Countries
SCIA	Supreme Council of Islamic Affairs
SCSN	Supreme Council for Sharia in Nigeria
SSS	State Security Services
TC	*Today's Challenge*
TCNN	Theological College of Northern Nigeria
TD	*ThisDay*
TEKAN	Tarayyar Ekklisiyoyin Kristi a Nigeria (Fellowship of the Churches of Christ in Nigeria)
VS	*Vancouver Sun*
WB	World Bank
WT	*Weekly Trust*
9/11	Attack on the World Trade Center on September 11, 2001

Foreign Words

Almajirai	Pupils of Qur'anic schools (Hausa)
Hajj	Pilgrimage (Arabic)
Hijab	Approved women's garb (Arabic)
Hijira	Migration of Prophet to Medina (Hausa, Arabic)
Imam	Leader of mosque (Arabic)
Jihad	Holy War (Arabic)
Mea culpa	My fault (Latin)
Sharia	Muslim law (Arabic)
Umma	Muslim community (Arabic)

▲ ONE

INTRODUCTION

The decades of religious bloodbaths in Nigeria are well-known. They have received wide publicity in the international media. Locally, these events have almost become the bread and butter for Nigerian journalists by providing them with a long list of sensational cover stories.

The riots themselves are the subject of Monograph One, *Nigeria's Decades of Blood,* where they are described in lurid detail. The monograph you now have at hand, Volume Two of the series *Studies in Christian–Muslim Relations,* assumes familiarity with these events and does not repeat or even summarize them. An adequate appreciation of this present volume therefore requires familiarity with the flow of events as recorded in Monograph One.

What are the causes of the violent flare-ups in Nigeria? That is the question for this monograph. In Monograph One, the emphasis is primarily on the flow of the events themselves, the "facts," if you will. In this monograph, the primary focus is on opinion and interpretation—so you are asked to listen; to take it all in. Absorb the major opinions, including the strong emotions in which they are often wrapped. Leave your critical faculties in abeyance during your initial reading. Try to feel along with these opinions and views. Sometimes their relationship to the facts on the ground is not immediately clear. More specifically, Monograph Two describes major Muslim views; Monograph Three is going to be devoted to Christian opinions.

It is risky to peg everyone. Where, for example, do I put reporters and journalists associated with the government-owned *New Nigerian;* or the private newsmagazine *National Concord,* founded by the late Moshood Abiola, in life one of Nigeria's most prominent and wealthy Muslim businessmen and politicians? Who is Christian or Muslim? I am reduced to picking and choosing my way on basis of names, since these can be telling in Nigeria, but not in a foolproof way. So, in the process, I fully expect to displease some by placing them in the wrong category. I am sorry about that. I will try my best. Sometimes, you have only a choice between doing nothing and taking risks. I choose the risk and apologize ahead of time for some inevitable mistakes.

Familiarity with Volume One is also helpful for some other reasons. For one, it contains the Introduction to the entire series. It is there that I explain that I do not always follow strict academic convention in this study, though it is based on responsible research and thirty years' experience. In addition, I explain my footnote policy and some other issues there. In the meantime, my footnotes have changed somewhat. Apart from those that contain text, I now provide just enough information so that you can identify the author and publication by checking the Bibliography.

An important part of the Introduction in Volume One is the explanation of the perspective with which I operate, namely that of Kuyperianism, a wholistic version of Christianity that has closer parallels to the wholism of Islam than any other Christian school of thought of which I am aware.

Then there is the promise of a companion CD-Rom. In addition to the text of these volumes, that disk will eventually include some rare official documents and other writings from both Christian and Muslim sources for which there is no room in these volumes. That companion volume may well become an important resource on Christian–Muslim relations for Sub-Saharan Africa. Having both Volume One and the CD-Rom at hand will enhance your reading of the paper volume.[1]

The parties whose opinions and views are reflected in these pages cover a wide range. I cover religious, academic, journalistic, and political opinions, but also include the opinions of "ordinary" people who write letters to editors. These are opinions that emerge from the hearts of their authors. They represent the heart-felt hurts of the common people, less spoiled by the corrupt motivations of most politicians and other elite. I consider them to contain the most honest expressions of Christian and Muslim piety—even if they have been deceived by elite manipulators.

It should be understood, of course, that neither Muslims nor Christians always agree with their fellow adherents. The opinions of some Muslim academics, for example, can differ markedly from those of Muslim Activists, my term for Fundamentalists. Like their Christian counterparts in Nigeria, Muslim academics are sometimes influenced by Marxism. Even Muslim Activists sometimes disagree with each other as in the case of the Governor of Zamfara State, who launched the current sharia[2] campaign, and El-Zakzaky,[3] both prominent Nigerian Muslim activists about whom we will hear more. The post-September 11—or as it is now commonly dubbed, "9/11"—situation has demonstrated clearly that, like Christianity, Islam presents many faces, not infrequently contradictory ones. This situation is not a negative complaint; it is a challenge that arises from the complexity of both religions and, in fact, all of reality, none of which can be captured in clearly-defined boxes.

This monograph summarizes major Muslim opinions about Nigeria's religious violence. I quote so many Muslims that the reader could occasionally forget that I am a Christian. However, I cannot deny myself. My Christian self, including my religion and personality, will occasionally assert itself. I promise to keep that to a minimum to such an extent that some Christian readers may well consider me a traitor. I challenge such Christians. I want you to hear the Muslim voice. Consider it sympathetically. Put yourself in their shoes. Feel along with them. Listening is not a well-developed Nigerian skill; screaming is more highly developed. But I demand from Christians: Listen—listen carefully! In the next monograph, I will make the same demand on Muslims. Without people carefully listening to each other, Nigeria's religious problem will not be solved; screaming and violence will only make it worse.

I repeat my invitation to Muslims to pay close attention to this series of monographs as it develops. I promise that I will not offer you the usual diet offered by Christian apologists that you often regard as diatribe. You will find surprising Christian–Muslim parallels. To be sure, I will not hesitate to criticize you where you deserve it or advise you to compromise where rigidity could lead to disaster. At the same time, you will find in these pages unaccustomed appreciation for your stand on issues like sharia, religion as a total way of life, the human calling and secularism. Come, let us walk it together.

▲ Notes

[1] For example, the current version of the CD contains Vol. 2 as well as a penultimate and longer version of Vol. 3 long before the paper edition appears. It also contains my article on the aborted 2002 Miss World pageant in Nigeria along with quite a number of articles by Nigerians on the subject. It will continue to expand well beyond this paper version. Updated versions will be made available at discount prices. Though much is being published about Islam these days, very little is available about the contemporary situation in Black Africa, where both Christianity and Islam are on the march and in vigorous competition with each other.

[2] "Sharia" is an Arabic term used in this book to refer to Muslim law. In this series, it is such a household word that I will treat it as an English word. The concept will be defined and explained in depth in a later monograph.

[3] This is to put you on notice that Nigerian names often have variant spellings. That of El-Zakzaky is no exception.

▲ TWO

HISTORICAL BACKGROUND

For some decades now, a new revivalist spirit has bestirred the hearts of the global Muslim *ummah*, the community. It has not bypassed the Nigerian Muslim community. This spirit has created a new self-awareness that is a major key to understanding the issues of this volume and, indeed, of the entire series. That revivalist spirit is, as will be obvious throughout, extremely upbeat, self-affirming, self-righteous and very angry. I undertake to do my very best to explain that spirit accurately and with as much empathy as I can muster. I will try to restrain my critical faculty, especially in this current chapter, and hope that Muslims recognize themselves in the picture about to unfold. I ask my fellow Christians to walk and feel along with them, also subduing their critical attitude and anger for a few moments.

▲ Colonial Undermining of the Muslim Foundation

This chapter presents you with a resume of some major themes in Nigerian Muslim historiography as reconstructed by the revivalist spirit. By reconstruction I do not mean to imply that they have reconstructed the "facts"of that history so much as the colonial interpretation of these "facts." I could have said "as rewritten"or even "as corrected." I do in fact hold that their interpretation of that history is more accurate than the colonial version—more accurate, not fully accurate, for it is marked by exaggeration, and by an imputation of motives that is often off the mark.

It is with deep love, pride, and considerable nostalgia that Nigerian Muslims look upon the early 19th-century "Jihadist Movement"[1] that led to the revivalist empire of Shehu Usman Dan Fodio. That empire became famous as the Sokoto Caliphate. As the politically correct version has it, prior to Dan Fodio's militant revival campaign, the northern Nigerian Muslim community was in a degenerate state. It was marked by "flagrant abuse of the sharia by the venal scholars as well as by the greedy, oppressive and ignorant nominal Muslim kings. As to the majority of the people, knowledge of the true teachings of Islam was almost non-existent." "Syncretism was the order of the day and Islam was almost entirely confined to dry rituals. In the social, political and economic spheres, Islam was not allowed to interfere."[2] Rulers and religious leaders "conspired to erect a thick wedge between the masses and the true Islamic teachings.... The total picture... was very dark."[3] That is the general Muslim opinion of the pre-Fodio degenerate Muslim climate at the end of the 19th century in Sokoto country.

Shehu Dan Fodio instituted a radical revival that had its effect on every aspect of the culture. Many of the papers in Rashid's compilation of conference papers can be regarded as a tribute to Shehu's restoration of a glorious Muslim empire in which the comprehensive justice of sharia was implemented in all its beautiful fullness.

It is not only Muslim scholars in Rashid's book who have high regard for Dan Fodio. The pages of more recent popular Muslim-oriented newspapers and magazines are replete with references to the Shehu and admiration for him. In the current sharia-focused climate, the history of sharia in Nigeria that is considered relevant usually starts with Dan Fodio as both the beginning and the standard to which many Muslims, even the rebellious Muslim Students Association, want to return.[4] Articles with systematic analyses of his thoughts, whether theological or political, appear in some newspapers on a somewhat regular basis. His flag is on display in a museum. There is/was an institute named after him in Katsina, while the University of Sokoto has recently been renamed after him. The Governor of Zamfara State, who started the current campaign for sharia, has more than once been dubbed a modern Dan Fodio, a compliment higher than which is hardly possible.[5] Dan Fodio was a major watershed in Nigerian Muslim history. His reputation is based on the claim that he restored Islam by establishing a political order according to the sharia. And then the British came in 1900 to spoil it all.

Though Lord Lugard, the founder and first governor of the new British colony of Northern Nigeria, promised not to interfere in the Muslim religion,[6] he in fact interfered massively by setting into motion a process that deeply undermined Islam and led to serious deterioration of the Muslim spirit. The fact that he himself may not have realized this should not surprise us. He made this promise from his secular perspective that hardly grasps the comprehensive nature of the religion that formed the foundation of the society. He did not realize that when he inaugurated changes in the judicial system, he was in fact seriously interfering in Islam and thus breaking his promise.

The effect was serious. As Rashid puts it:

> *The dynamic policy towards the administration of Islamic law advocated by Uthman Fodio and others has become stagnant and static under the influence of colonialism and neo-colonialism. The emphasis has shifted from the "social relevance" and "public good" of laws, a hallmark of Maliki jurisprudence, to their so-called "modernisation," which simply means their*

> *conformity to Western legal values. It was indeed mischievous that Islamic law was allowed to be applied only so long as it was not found "repugnant to natural justice, equity and good conscience..." ...without any regard to the fact that the English statute...could itself be "repugnant...."*[7]

The major complaint is that colonialism brought three basic changes to Dan Fodio's perfect legacy and thereby ruined it. It reduced the scope of the sharia, introduced the foreign and abhorrent repugnancy concept, and inserted the demonic virus of secularism. The details of these changes belong more properly in Volume 4 of this series and will thus be treated there. However, for this volume it is important to realize the strength and depth of the Muslim sense of humiliation and oppression that underlies much of Nigeria's violence. They have been deprived of the most precious gift of Allah and been forced to submit to a foreign secular system repugnant to them. The process set into motion by Lugard acted like a drug that put the Muslim community off guard and undermined their religion.

The result of an entire century of Western interference and domination is a Muslim society in disarray. Laments Bello Sakkwato, "Muslims are aware of the desire of the West/secular states...to vanquish the Islamic ideology" and of the ways in which they pursue their goals, mostly by "deceit, treachery, dictatorship and many punitive means which include political, economic, etc., against Muslims states and peoples."[8] The Nigerian situation is merely a chapter of the international scene. Its sentiments are representative of the wider *ummah*. An Evangelical Press report quotes Hassan Turabi, described as "Sudan's Islamic leader,"as saying "America incarnates the devil for Muslims. When I say 'Muslims,' I mean all the Muslims in the world"—and that from one who obtained his doctorate from a cradle of Western sophistication, the Sorbonne. Another example of the international attitude is Zafar

Bangash, Director of the Institute of Contemporary Islamic Thought, who summarizes the common picture many Muslims around the globe have "of the true nature of the US, and why Imam Khomeini memorably called it 'shaytan-e buzurg'—the great Satan." He writes:

> *The title "rogue superpower," or "shaytan-e buzurg" in Imam Khomeini's celebrated phrase, commonly used for the US, is not merely political rhetoric; it is the deeply felt and perceptive view of people wounded by America's crude and arrogant policies. What is even more revealing is that these feelings are not confined to those directly targeted by Uncle Sam; even its European allies have started to feel uneasy about the uncouth behaviour of the overbearing uncle.*[9]

Another Evangelical Press report, already back in 1998, warned of Bin Laden's intentions. He is to have said that "We, with God's help, call on every Muslim who believes in God and wishes to be rewarded to comply with God's order to kill the Americans and plunder their money wherever and whenever they find it."[10] From there it was not very far to the World Trade Center in New York. And from similar perches in Nigeria it was not very far to Kano, Katsina, Maiduguri, Kaduna, Jos, Kafanchan, Zangon Kataf and all the other Nigerian cities that hosted riots.

Exceptions, it is said, prove the rule. Though the above attitude is nearly universal in Nigeria, R. D. Abubakre of the University of Ilorin does not share it. We will soon see that the common attitude puts colonialism and Christian missions in one basket, but Abubakre insists on a distinction. "Many British officials," he wrote, "were sympathetic towards the Muslims," certainly more than "many present Nigerian non-Muslims." The one and only illustration he adduces is the help they rendered to improve education for Muslims, the details of which follow below in the section on that subject.[11]

In our post-9/11 world, Westerners have become somewhat familiar with the "satanic view" many Muslims throughout the world have of the West, especially the USA. It is too bad Westerners were not sufficiently aware of it before, since it has a history of several decades, even at grassroots level in Nigeria. Alas, as one I. I. Bello put it in a letter to the editor:

> *An American citizen is virtually cut from the realities of the world. He is turned into an arrogant speck of dust. He is made to believe that whatever American leadership did...is absolutely right. He is deprived of any standard of moral value or judgement. He is robbed of the spirituality of his humanity and made to believe [that] only his material aspect matters, and by so doing [is] reduced [to] the level of a beast, a mere consumer. These "achievements"—as the helpless American citizen is made to believe—have been accomplished by the endless nights of plotting and planning of the Jewish-controlled American mass media.*[12]

For good measure, but to prevent overkill in the main text, I attach Appendix 1, which is a longer and typical Nigerian Muslim statement about America that needs to be understood and taken seriously. Since it was written, Western awareness of this attitude has grown to the point of familiarity due to post-9/11 events, but whether there is any Western awareness of its partial truth and significance remains to be seen. The dominant Western attitude I see is one of smug contempt for radical nonsense that is mostly shrugged off.

I rush to attach two warnings to this appendix. The first is that American missionaries should become more aware of their image as representatives of this "shaitan," while their Canadian counterparts, whether they like it or not, should realize they are usually tarred with the same brush, because they look and sound the same. Both would do themselves and Nigeria a favour by looking for serious ways to disassociate themselves clearly from this image. Such disassociation cannot be achieved by a mere change in window dressing: It will require a process of conscientization and a serious shift in emphasis in their message.

The second warning is that the time is past that such statements can be ignored. Ignoring them in the past has led to 9/11. Ignoring them in the future will only generate more terrorism and possibly World War III. Both Nigerian and Western governments, along with their churches and citizens, had better listen to these statements and change their ways with Muslims by taking them seriously and respecting their religion. If these warnings sound like a personal aside from me, your author, they are also expressive of the global Muslim attitude.[13]

▲ Subversion of Muslim Communities and Institutions

By now it should be clear that, according to Muslim opinion, colonialism not only undermined the legal setup of the sharia, but it "unhinged"or deranged Muslim society as a whole—and not only Muslim society. The entire Nigerian society in all of its cultural aspects is said to have degenerated into unprecedented depths of vice and immorality. Sani A. Ibrahim, holder of a highly prestigious traditional Kano title, towards the end of the era covered by this study, affirmed that "ever since the Europeans entered the country, they have tried to destroy the good culture of the Hausa people. Even after independence, they have continued to send us their literature and movies that promote the evil customs of Europeans among us." [14]

It is an unending litany. As Sakkwato summarizes it, "One cannot fail to recognise that the breakdown of morality, social order, peace and progress in this country was sown since the sacking of the caliphate...."[15] The former military head of state, Muhammadu

Buhari, summed it up: It was from Sokoto "that the colonialists started the encroachment on Islam and our traditions."[16]

This theme forms a common thread through all of Nigerian Muslim social writings ever since the Constituent Assembly of the 70s. It would take very little effort to fill several volumes describing the social, economic, political, health care, sexual, religious, legal/judicial, and moral degredation that Muslims blame on the colonial and post-colonial setups. In this section I describe a number of areas in which Muslims feel they are cheated, oppressed, or manipulated by the Christo-secular government establishment Nigeria inherited from the colonialists. It will be enough to give you a strong flavour of the anger, humiliation and both patience and impatience Muslims have been suffering for some decades.

▲ Distorted Governments

Not only was the Muslim mind deeply distorted by colonialism and its post-colonial local house boys, but so were the structures of society, especially the various governments in the country. The governments and other power structures that God ordained for Muslims have been hijacked by those *kafirai* who have established a satanic network of Christian secularism and international capitalism that is working to destroy the global *ummah* of Allah. Due to all of this, the country is sinking deeper and deeper into a morass of unprecedented immorality that continues to undermine the very foundation of Islam. The entire country is organized by Christians and their agents in the government to oppress and squeeze Islam on all sides.

The signs of this oppression are everywhere. Muslims never imposed their law on their non-Muslim subjects, according to an anonymous writer, an assertion backed up by references to Muslim rule over Jews and over Hindus.[17] But in Nigeria, Christians oppose everything Muslim. Umaru Dembu, an official of Jama'tul Nasril Islam (JNI) from Zaria, "expressed regret" that Christians had "formed the habit of opposing anything which would be of benefit to Nigeria if it had something to do with the Islamic religion."[18] Even the irenical R. D. Abubakre charges that "there is a tendency among Nigerian non-Muslims to be subjective in their criticism of the institutions of Islam. They criticise *hajj* indiscriminately and condemn fasting." If they were to ponder Muslim practices more sympathetically, they would have recognized the parallels in their own religion. When Ahmadu Bello, the famous Sardauna or Sultan of Sokoto, became Vice President of the Muslim World League in the early 1960s, Christians "through sustained mass communication media propaganda gave it severe criticism." This occurred even though they had their own Francis Akanu Ibiam, former Governor of the Eastern Region, who was "a leading member of a World Christian organisation" that is not further identified. Abubakre complains that though "Islam and Christianity have mountainous areas of convergence," they are "least emphasized." Instead, Christians ignore these "mountainous areas of convergence" as if they are mere "mole hills," while they turn points of divergence into mountains.[19] In Nigeria, "it is only Christians that exercise their rights without limitations." Muslims, on the other hand, "are denied their rights...in the name of secularism."[20]

It is not only secularism that leads to deprivation of Muslim rights. There are also factors like tribalism, jealousy and just plain hatred of Muslims that rear their ugly heads. Sometime in 1987, a large crowd of Bachama people from over 25 villages descended on the Hausa people living in the villages of Tinno and Tito in the Numan Local Government area and killed over 50 of them. In addition, they burnt their houses, crops and machinery. What was not destroyed, they confiscated and took to their own villages. The Bachama are mostly Traditionalists and Christians, Lutherans to be exact.

As Dangogo[21] tells the story, these Hausa people hailed from various northern states and had lived in the Numan area for some forty to fifty years. They were a law-abiding people, peaceful and industrious. Furthermore, they had always treated the local Bachama people with respect. However, jealousy set in amongst the Bachama when they noticed that these strangers soon became more prosperous than the locals. It was this jealousy that set in motion increasing friction between the two groups. The Yola television station, manned by Bachama, began to put their Hausa "guests" in a bad light, as if they had no right to live there. This, claimed Dangogo, is in stark contrast to what exists in their states of origin where there are Bachama who live there in peace without molestation.

Another early sign of trouble was that the Bachama put a "jizyar,"[22] or poll tax on the Hausa farmers' harvest that went to the Bachama chief. Though unhappy, the Hausa people paid the tax. However, that was not the idea of the Bachama, who really intended that the Hausa would leave the area. Then a number of Bachama began to claim the Hausa farms as theirs, even though the Hausa had allegedly received their plots from an earlier chief and had to start from scratch by clearing uninhabited and uncultivated land. Those farms had belonged to no one and no one had to be moved or give up his property. Yet these Bachama said these farms had only been lent to them. Just in the village of Tinno, 650 farms were illegally confiscated. When the village chief of Waduku disagreed with this land grabbing, he was promptly killed along with his brother.

The Hausa took the matter to the Bachama Chief, but he supported his own people and berated the Hausa as an ungrateful people who had arrived in poverty, but now that they had become wealthy they wanted to take over power in the area. When the Hausa then went on to the police who are not local, some of them were arrested for causing trouble. They then went to the local court but, since it was dominated by the Bachama, they received no support. The next step was to contact the chairperson of the local government, Stella Manset, also a Bachama. She "chased them away, calling them 'strangers' and asking when they had come to take over local farmland."[23] Even an appeal to the state government yielded no solution, since the people assigned to report to the government were the same chief and chairperson. However, as the situation deteriorated and violence began to escalate, the state government established a committee to serve them with advice. The committee tendered its report in December, 1987, but by July, 1988, the government had not taken any action. The Hausa people were attacked more and more. At one time a contingent of a mere fifty police had to face a crowd of over 4,000 Bachama who had come with army-type weapons. It was eventually the army that broke it up and restored a kind of normalcy—a familiar story in Nigerian confrontations. As far as Muslims are concerned, we have here a case of a local people in tandem with almost every level of government oppressing a non-indigenous group of Hausa Muslims.

Apart from the article on which the above story is based, I have not succeeded in finding any other references to this fracas except in a letter of February 9, 1989, by Wilson Sabiya to Governor Isah Mohammed of Gongola State that will constitute part of an appendix in Volume Three. That letter suggests that Governor Mohammed sponsored write-ups in the *New Nigerian* against both the Gongola State branch of CAN and Mohammed's predecessor, Governor David Jang, the Christian governor in charge during this episode. These write-ups alleged that CAN and Jang had collaborated against these Hausa Muslims to kill and maim them.

Probably one of the worst places from the Muslim point of view is Plateau State, sometimes considered the Christian headquarters in the north, a thorn in the northern Muslim flesh. Though it claims a reputation as a peaceful state, it was the scene of two bitter riots in 1994 and in 2001 and since then has moved into a mode of perpetual violence and murder. Muslims accuse this state of discrimination on many fronts.

Among others, there is their infamous *Nigeria Standard (NS)*, a daily owned by the state government and established at least partially to defend itself and its indigenous Christian population against Muslim encroachment. An anonymous writer referred to "the Jos Christian Mafia" and "its crusading voice, the *Nigeria Standard*."[24] One Adamu Ibrahim, in a letter to the editor, accused the paper of a strong bias towards Christians and against Muslims. While it featured a Christian column, he missed its Muslim counterpart. He reminded the editor that it operates on government funds that belong to everybody, a dangerous situation in a state with an equal number of Muslims and Christians. The editor responded by wondering whether Ibrahim reads the Friday edition which has a regular Muslim column.[25] It is a minor issue, but Ibrahim's letter is an indication how ready Muslims are with the charge of discrimination and oppression without even a superficial glance at the facts—but, of course, they are not the only ones.

The Pen took up the Muslim case against Plateau. It reported that the local JNI complained against various offences by *NS*. A particularly gross offence was that insulting anti-Muslim cartoon.[26] The report further asserted, "The Standard has been the strongest anti-Islamic and anti-Hausa/Fulani establishment newspaper, even though it is funded by the public treasury. The JNI cited a provocative anti-Islamic article published in the Sunday Standard [27] which was carried to intimidate the Muslim populace."

The same Plateau JNI leader had his complaints about the state's radio and TV services with their bias against Islam:

> *Christian programmes are aired daily while the Muslims are given only 30 minutes a week (every Friday)! The state radio, however, allows a five-minute prayer time in the morning for the Muslims, which used to be 15 minutes. He mentioned in particular "700 Club"and "Another Life,"all Christian-sponsored programmes aired daily on television against the wishes of the dominant Muslims in the state. When the Muslims requested for*

> *the same airtime for their programmes, among which were videotapes of Ahmed Deedat, they were turned down on the grounds that it is a controversial series and that even if a substitute is provided, the air time has already been sold.*[28]

The accusations against Plateau State with its Christian establishment just go on and on. There is "the growing under-representation of Muslims in the government, irrespective their numerical superiority, at least according to the 1963 census. There are only four Muslims in the state Executive Council. Equally there is an average of only one Muslim permanent secretary out of every five Christians in that position." [29]

As if all of this were not enough, *The Pen* accused the people of Plateau of developing anti-Muslim militarism. Under the heading "Jos: Islam under Fire—Muslims Cry out," Christians in Plateau State are now alleged to be undergoing paramilitary training in various places in preparation for a possible religious war with the Muslims:

> *...Students and voluntary organisations now freely use dummy guns or locally made ones in training. It has also been noticed that Christian leaders, organisations and institutions are now fortifying their houses and compounds to provide cover and security for their nefarious activities.*
>
> *Apart from their daily preparation for an eventual showdown, the Christians are now engaged in offensive open-air preaching in spite of edicts banning open-air preaching.... To further provoke Muslims, they choose the main road leading to the central mosque as their "open-air church."*[30]

A controversy arose in Plateau State about mosques. Muslims had built mosques in various public places like markets, taxi parks, hospitals, government buildings and others. Then Christians, in a bid for equal treatment, began demanding plots from the government so they could also build churches there. The late Paul Gindiri, a wealthy businessman as well as a colourful, fearless, and aggressive evangelist, built a church in the middle of the Bauchi Motor Park. He started similar moves at the Polo Ground. Faced with this demand, the Christian Military Governor, Lawrence Onoja, announced that all places of worship in public places would be destroyed so as to get rid of the problem. Muslims strongly objected to this solution, for they correctly realized that this measure would only affect them, since Christians normally had neither churches in public places nor any need for them. However, Muslims claimed they do need them since they pray five times a day wherever they are. So, the order to demolish such houses of worship was received by Muslims as another Plateau attempt to destroy Islam. As so often is the case, this issue was immediately placed in a larger contextual framework of other anti-Muslim measures in the state, such as the alleged military training at schools, Christian favourite treatment by Plateau media, and others.[31]

Editorial "Comment" from *The Pen* supported the complaints of *Alkalami*, its Hausa-language twin, forcefully, with ill-concealed threats. It declared the order "the most reckless and dangerous instruction by any governor in this administration." It was merely "a cover-up...to simply phase out towering mosques that abound everywhere in Plateau state." It was "the greatest spectre of doom." That the governor withdrew the order—"shameless eaten up his words"—was none of the Muslims' business. The "power drunk and crisscrossed governor"is warned that Muslims are "now prepared to take up any challenge, irrespective of his perceived power." The Muslims are "law abiding, peace loving and honest to all," but they "can no longer fold their arms." The governor is reminded that, according to the 1963 census, Islam is the majority religion in the state. The editor, "assisting the government to avert an impending holocaust," reminds it "that so many incidents and calamities against the Muslims are still fresh in our memories." Then he lists some: The OIC issue, the "Kafanchan massacre, unguarded provocations by CAN leaders." There were the "recent Numan genocide, the clandestine moves to stifle *hajj* operations and the indiscriminate arrests and detention without trial of Muslim youths and their leaders." He further warned that "efforts should be made to right the wrongs already committed and to ensure justice and fairness in the future.[32] Clearly, many Muslims do not think of Plateau as so peaceful. They find it an oppressive place, which is, I understand, the main reason the Lafia and surrounding areas broke off to form their own Muslim-dominated state of Nasarawa.

It should be pointed out that the Plateau media are not the only ones accused of anti-Muslim discrimination. It is thought to be the case with most of the nation's media. The Lagos-based Muslim magazine *Al-Madinah* reported a bizzarre "Mother of All Miracles" that was considered so important that, even though the current issue had already been fully prepared, the editor decided to start from scratch to report the event. Reportedly a small snail emerged from the Atlantic Ocean at Lagos' Bar Beach with an Arabic inscription on its shell affirming Allah and His prophet Muhammad. If humans "turn deaf ears to the true message, forces of nature now take it upon themselves to proclaim the miracle of Islam," declared the editor. It was *Al-Madinah*'s duty to spread this wonderful news, for "apart from NTA[33] Newsline which grudgingly flashed it, we are not aware of any other coverage in any Nigeria media, print or electronic. We also know why: It is simply because the discovery is a feather in the cap of Islam. Al-Madinah knows its duty, though. And it has to do it." [34]

So, a strong sense of Muslim media mission in the face of an anti-Muslim media establishment.[35]

The complaints about the media have continued all along the way, as recent as March, 2003, when Nasiru A. Yahya of Jalingo, the capital of Taraba State, wrote about anti-Muslim discrimination by Taraba Television. It has deteriorated "into a Christian propaganda station." He explained:

Christian programmes are offered a regular and comprehensive coverage. The most pathetic part is that even on Fridays, the Muslim sermon enjoys only 30 minutes, while after that, a Christian programme or gospel music follows immediately. More so, transmission opens with gospel music and closes with it, instead of prayers.

Furthermore, during any Christian occasion, a comprehensive coverage is broadcast from various Christian churches, while important events concerning Muslims are blacked out. Moreover, after every programme, the interlude is a gospel music, which exhibits the worst form of religious discrimination.

I can state here without any hesitation that the Muslim community in the state constitutes a significant percentage of the state's population, but because of Muslim peace-loving attitude, we don't usually protest the discrimination. Nevertheless, we wouldn't be taken for granted, for it is becoming unpalatable, and action must be taken.

For your information, all that has been spent on the station was supposedly for the benefit of both Muslims and Christians in the state. Because of the alienation and discrimination, the Muslim ummah is losing interest and many have decided not to tune to the station. I call on all those concerned to redress the situation in the interest of peace and unity in the state.[36]

Betrayal by Emirate and Other Muslim Authorities

There is friction also within the Muslim community with one section accusing the other of having been colonized and secularized. Muslim emirs and chiefs are accused of exactly that. Remember that some of the riots in Volume One were directed at least partially against them. One issue that crops up frequently, especially in Fundamentalist writings, is that Muslim emirs and lower-rank chiefs have betrayed their people. This was alleged to be the case before the Dan Fodio revival[37] and once again became the case under colonialism. Emirs and chiefs retained their position and received favours by playing their assigned roles under the colonial policies of indirect rule and secularism.

It is a complaint that comes from all levels of society. One Sadik Jahun from Birnin Kudu sent in advice to MAMSER, a Federal Government agency assigned to wake up the Nigerian population from their slumber and develop themselves. His advice was that the agency should work closely with various estates in the society, such as the press, educational establishments and religious leaders. However, he warned that MAMSER should stay clear of traditional chiefs. "These chiefs have lost their respect with the people and are not interested in arousing them. Politics has separated them from the people." He warned to keep away from them, "unless MAMSER were to try to return them to their former position" by reforming the institution.[38]

Hassan Gadam, a civil servant in Bauchi State, one who was probably very familiar with all the corruption for which the Nigerian civil service is famous, wrote a lengthy cry to Muslim traditional rulers and authorities in the civil service. He pleaded with them to live up to their Muslim obligations by fulfilling the roles to which Allah had assigned them. Failure to do so would lead to judgement. "I am calling on all of you,"he wrote, "who fail to do their work according to the Word of God. You share one common destination: the fire of hell, unless you repent before you die. Thus, you chiefs and high officials, do justice and accord everyone his rights without restrictions." [39]

His article is full of accusations that these people use their positions to their own advantage, and in the process oppress the people and ignore the laws of God.[40]

Bobboyi, at the time at North Western University in Chicago, reports that the colonial yoke weighed so heavily on them that highly-placed Muslim rulers seriously discussed resorting to *hijira*. The source is a letter from Muhammadu Buhari, Sarkin Kano Aliyu, to the Waziri of Sokoto, two highly-placed officials in the traditional Muslim setup during the early colonial period. The former suggested seriously that Muslims should resort to the *hijira*, a traditional Muslim concept of fleeing an intolerable situation by moving away. The letter states, "I have found no more useful plan for all Muslims...that we leave this country, all of us...as these dogs have surrounded us and threaten to overcome us."[41] This is a clear indication how deeply the secular colonial order disturbed their spirits. If they were to remain true Muslims, they could have no peace with it.

The flight never materialized, partially because colonialism soon succeeded in undermining the Muslim spirit amongst these rulers. Pragmatism set in. Muslim rulers began to find ways to exploit the new order for their own benefit. During the course of this discussion on *hijira*, Muhammadu Marafa, who was Sultan of Sokoto from 1915-1924, "did not hide his feelings" to his predecessor, Sultan Attahiru. He wrote:

> *Further, I earnestly beseech you, in God's name, let no one hear a suggestion of our departure from your mouth in this land, as this would mean ruin of our affairs. Our subjects...would certainly throw off their allegiance to us on hearing such news. We should get no assistance from them of what they have promised to us. To sum up, let us sit and wait the issue of the matter...If we remain in our Kingdom, all will be ordered for us by the Great Ordainer.*[42]

A pragmatism had begun to set in that eventually led to a betrayal of the people by the ruling class. Bobboyi explains that "the incorporation of traditional Muslim institutions" into the secular colonial system led to autocracy. The Emir was now accountable to the British, not to the people, as before, or to the sharia. He and the British Resident would have their huddle and decide "as they saw fit." "[A] wide gulf developed between the Islamic pretensions of the Emirs and their actual deeds; between the ideals and aspirations of a Muslim society and the temporal exigencies of a secular-colonial arrangement...."[43]

And so Bashir Isyaku laments that:

> *...the vitality of the Sultanate has been eroded since the demise of its founder, and probably one could argue that it has now been brought to its feet. The honour and respect accorded to the institution has since been lost to history as it is now more of a Government mouthpiece to mobilize the Muslims into casting their vote...supporting government programmes like MAMSER, announcing the sighting of specific moons and appealing for calm when there is any civil disorder....One would...therefore wonder whether it is necessary any longer to lament the plight of such an institution.*[44]

Simultaneous with the unrest about the Sokoto Sultanate, Kano was the scene of the 25th anniversary celebration of the enthronement of its Emir Ado Bayero. The editors of both *The Pen* and its twin *Alkalami* were hardly in the mood for such a celebration; it was rather a time for mourning because of the deterioration of the emirate position.[45] The *Alkalami* editor reminds the Emir of his heavy responsibilities as "leader of the people in both politics and religion...as well as to serve as an example for the people in the way of truth." The most important function for the "Emir of Kano and all other Muslim chiefs, is to protect the sharia and to ensure that the freedom of Muslims is not tampered with. In short, they are to enhance the position of both Muslims and their religion."[46]

However, laments *The Pen*, instead of emirs defending the supremacy of Islam and the welfare of their people, "nothing significant remains of the caliphate and its leaders." It goes on to complain that Emirs receive their appointments from neo-colonial, non-Muslim governments, both civilian and military, and are thus forced "to pay homage and allegiance to such regimes." They "were to mobilise and lead their people to fight for Islam," but they are reduced to enjoining their people to keep mute, and accepting a leadership that recognises not the Islam that made them, as the supreme religion, and the sharia as the only way of life. It is sad to note that, despite the Muslim demand for his right to sharia, the emirs never at any moment cared to use their influential position to make a strong case in favour of the sharia to the government that recognises them. Secularism and its attendant institutions continue to flourish in the domains of our emirs without a single move to stem its tide by the blue-blooded royalists.

The editor of *Alkalami* expressed himself even stronger. "Every chief must unite his people to show them what will bring them progress and to resist everything to the contrary. Doing so will bring the chief and his people closer together so that they will respect him more highly and he receive an appropriate reward from God." [47]

The point here is that the stark opposite is in fact the case. The original assignment to these Muslim chiefs from Shehu Dan Fodio himself was to "resist everything that is not according to Islam and to serve as faithful stewards of the Lord God on earth. Thus, they must fight against oppression and against the arrangements of the colonialists and others who try to force pagan law on Muslims." [48]

The editor of the same issue of *Alkalami* was so over-wrought with the oppressive situation that he wrote two editorials on the subject in one edition, both touching on the same basic concern for Muslim liberation. In the editorial "Sharhin Alkalami," he bristled, "The insults, humiliation and the provocation to which Muslims have been subjected have long ago reached the limit of toleration."[49] The rest of this editorial deals mostly with sharia issues that will be examined more closely in the volume on sharia.

Now, if Muslim emirs and sultans have succumbed to the secular establishment, what could be expected of lesser Muslim mortals?

The impatience of Muslims towards the "system" has been growing at every front. We will see in Chapter Four that El-Zakzaky and the Muslim Students' Society (MSS) have long been very hostile to most Muslim authorities. The whole place has become one huge tinderbox continuously awaiting the next spark to be set off. It is obvious in the increasing resistance, especially of students to members of the secular establishment, even if they are Muslim.

In fact, it is becoming difficult to identify who is who and who favours what among Muslims. In November, 2002, it is alleged that "thugs assaulted two Islamic preachers," named Abdulrazaq Aduagba and Sannu Shehu. They were street preaching at midnight (!) in Ilorin. They are described as "outspoken Muslim preachers who have for some time been criticising the current trend of political violence in the state and the recent upgrading of traditional chiefs."

"Eye-witnesses" reported that "four heavily-built men bumped into the *wa'azi* (sermon) session, and produced Aduagba's recorded casette in which he criticised societal lapses, asking him to defend it. When he was trying to justify his thoughts, they rained blows on him, sending him to the floor before they took flight and boarded waiting Mercedes Benz and Toyota cars."[50] My guess is that we have a case here of an attack by established Muslim politicians on Fundamentalists who are challenging the status quo, including chieftaincy vested interests, and who thus stand in the tradition of *The Pen* and *Alkalami.* There is currently a dramatic increase in political violence in Nigeria. I would describe this last case as religious/political in nature—a political attack on religious critics of corrupt chiefs and social evils.

Secularized Education

I begin this section with some hard-hitting salvos against colonial education from Ibrahim K. R. Suleiman. He begins his discussion with a quotation from Edward Wilmot Blyden's description of the effect of colonial education on Africans. This quote sums it all up so well that I can do no better than to simply re-quote the passage. Blyden, it may surprise readers not familiar with Nigerian history, was a Christian, but one with a difference. He was a West Indian Pan-Africanist, active in West Africa during the closing decades of the 19th century and unusually supportive of Muslims. According to Abubakre, Blyden "was convinced that Muslims are not as bad as they were being projected by the missionaries." He fought their cause and encouraged Muslims to combine Islamic and Western education.[51] He wrote:

> *Of a different race, different susceptibility, different bent of character from that of the European, [the Africans] have been trained under influences in many respects adapted only to the Caucasian race. Christian and so-called civilised Negroes live in foreign countries, where they are only passive spectators of the deeds of a foreign race; and where, with other impressions which they receive from without, an element of doubt as to their own capacity. Hence, without the physical or mental aptitude for the enterprises which they are taught to admire and revere, they attempt to copy and imitate them and share the fate of all copyists and imitators. Bound to move on a lower level, they acquire and retain a practical inferiority, transcribing very often the faults, rather than the virtues, of their models.*
>
> *Besides the result of involuntary impressions, they often receive direct training which is not incompatible with, but destructive of, their self-respect. Having embraced, or at least assented to, these errors and falsehoods about himself, he concludes that his only hope of raising the scale of respectable manhood is to strive after whatever is most unlike himself and alien to his peculiar tastes. And whatever his literary attainments or acquired ability, he fancies that he must grind at the mill which is provided for him, putting in the materials fur-*

nished to his hand, bring no contribution from his own field, and of course, nothing comes out but what is put in it. He never acquires the self-respect or self-reliance of an independent contributor. He is not an independent help, only a subordinate help, so that the European feels that he owes no doubt and moves on in contemptuous indifferences of the Negro, teaching him to condemn himself.[52]

Blyden was right on. I myself have used another quote elsewhere to describe the purposes of colonial education by a highly respected advocate of colonialism, whose description, in fact, represented political correctness. H. S. Scott wrote,

The political conception of the aim of education was that it should make useful citizens...who would be of use to us [British]. The conception was one of exploitation and development for the benefit of...Great Britain—it was to this purpose that such education...was directed.[53]

In my own more negative terms, the purpose of education

was to produce zombies, creatures at the behest of the colonial regime, loyal, obedient, ready to do its bidding.... Least of all was it the intention to produce critical and creative graduates who would do independent thinking, for such people could become dangerous to the establishment.

An important part of the educational policy was that of special schools for the sons of chiefs and emirs. Among the consequences, if not the goals, was "the further entrenchment of Muslim chiefs and emirs and other northern aristocrats to whom Balarabe Musa later referred as 'crooks.'"[54] The above is a fair summary of the critical Muslim opinion of colonial education among Muslims.

In his hard-hitting article, Ibrahim K. R. Suleiman writes about "the enslavement"of Muslim "minds and intellect, and the arresting of our development as a people" that was "made possible through an educational system carefully designed to achieve those ends." He helps us overhear the Waziri of Sokoto, Alhaji Junaidu, addressing authorities at ABU and describing the place as "a cultural transplant whose roots lie in another tradition." Nigerian universities, he chided, belong "to us only in their location and in their names." The Nigerian Muslim world "has been put aside"; "African ideas and moral system" are ignored. He wonders how one can "understand or write about the events which have shaped this community without a serious study of the works of Shehu Dan Fodio" and other African Muslim classics.

"It is no wonder," Suleiman concludes, "that the universities only produce people who are contemptuous of their society." Their graduates "take pride in imitating the worst elements in Europe and America." Our scholars contribute to the process of giving the leadership to the West without their consciences being disturbed. He sadly decries that

> *What our students admire most are the dancehalls of Europe, the bubbling wines, the naked dances and perverted morals of Europe. They lack the will, the courage and the sincerity to make sacrifices for their own people and to offer devotional services for the betterment of the society. These 'fairest' elements of the society are also the most corrupt, most greedy, most immoral and shameless of all elements of the Nigerian Society. [Universities] have played a negative, if not destructive, role in our society. Unfitted themselves to our society, they produce students who are also unfit. They have failed naturally to command the respect and confidence of the very society they are to serve.*[55]

The MSS is seldom left behind in such discussions. An anonymous writer in their magazine presents us with a full dish of Muslim political correctness on the topic of education. The role of education "was to produce indigenes with the suitable mental disposition for the success of the colonial venture." The schools established among Muslims were to "de-Islamise and persuade the Muslim to forget about his Islam and submit to and participate in the...colonial machinery." They were to ensure that Muslim students "were sufficiently de-Islamised to accept to live under the English law instead of the sharia and to subscribe to Western, Euro-Christian thoughts and ideas." Thus a class was created of Christians and some Muslims who submitted to the regime. Such a person neither possesses the self confidence to see his worth, nor does he possess the courage to think outside the frame of his European mentor. The West to him represents both the ideal and the ultimate in wisdom and excellence. His yardstick is therefore the West, which he labours day in and day out to approximate. When his master saw no reason in staying any longer—for he can do the job more efficiently—the elite was well prepared to take over the imperialist machinery.

Members of the group neither questioned "the colonial arrangement nor were they asking for any fundamental changes in the status quo. They were, simply put, aspiring to step into the shoes of their white mentors and enjoy the privileges that had until then been the exclusive preserve of the white imperialists." Colonialists had achieved their goal. They "handed over power to safe hands; hands that will continue to preserve those same exploitative arrangements that they engineered; hands that will not venture to think outside the Western Euro-Christian frame of reference."

An important part of the educational programme is to allow "only Euro-Christian thoughts and ideas."

> *Islamic political thoughts, Islamic law, Islamic sociology, Islamic economics would not be tolerated, not because they don't exist but because they must not even be known to exist. The Muslims...are forced to learn that the only thoughts that*

exist are those of the Western Euro-Christian world. Islam has come to represent a target of hostility, a target to be vilified.[56]

Another anonymous writer in the same issue of *Radiance*—all writers in this issue are anonymous—writes in the same spirit:

The nature of the universities of the oppressed countries is designed to produce elites whose learned values are cultivated for the sake of continuing this oppression. There is no value system taught by our universities that is not totally alien to our culture. Thus, at the end, graduates come out as total aliens dedicated to imposing and protecting the oppressive status quo.[57]

The Pen does not disappoint us in this regard and generously serves us the same fare. Aliyu Dauda accuses "so-called third-world" universities (and by implication Nigerian), of producing "Europeanized natives or some kind of Americanized elite whose ideal in life is to become British, French, American or Russian." More, he calls their graduates

social misfits, as typified by the half-educated, quasi-intellectuals and mediocres as well as those suffering from mental slavery in the Western Euro-American bourgeois capitalist imperialism, or to that of the Eastern-Euro-Asian Marxist socialist confusionism.

He laments with Junaidu that the ideals of ABU, the North's premier university, "have clearly been perverted, bastardised and confused." It has become an environment totally alienated from the surrounding culture it is meant to stimulate. "The university's bogus, artificial, and alien environment and that of the modest and natural larger environment are opposed to each other."[58] Dauda further quotes from Junaidu, saying that "a truly universal view of human knowledge does not set out deliberately to eliminate a whole culture from the education of the children of that culture."

Dauda continues to complain that Nigerian academicians are "haughty and arrogant."

> *They are so arrogant and ideologically intoxicated that they condemn everything cherished by the very community which affectionately nurtured them, calling its ideals and social moral values "retrogressive," "conservative," "reactionary," "religious bigotry" and such garbage, as well as advocating for "change," "progress," "peace and stability" and similar nonsensical jargon.*

In reality, those graduates are merely the "house boys" of both West and East. The universities

> *have been gravely infected by most of the Western Euro-American societal moral ailments and the Eastern Euro-Asian cancer of atheistic indoctrination and other forms of deculturalization, dereligionization, dewomanization of women, and the dehumanisation of humanity.*

In order to achieve these "destructive satanic machinations," all sorts of "clubs, secret societies, women's 'liberation' associations, and Western imperialist-backed organisations and other dubious associations are daily being formed in order to subvert our national 'flag independence' and frustrate the revolutionary struggle of the Muslim *Ummah*."[59]

Abdul-Ghaniyy asserts that the West began to exploit the Muslim world from the 17th century onwards. Through the "dissemination of ideas and intrigues," colonialism initiated a "period of political decline and moral decadence." Education was their main tool. "Through this they succeeded in putting Western ideas and intrigues into Islamic books" and created bifurcated or dualistic mindsets that disabled Muslims from a legitimate understanding of Islam.

> *Thousands of Muslims...fell into this trap. Today, millions of Muslims are ready to practice Islam and do da'wah, but they*

> *are doing it with ignorance; they are overtaken by religious rigidity and stagnation, which is a result of intellectual immaturity, academic inadequacy and finally their philosophical absurdity. They are preaching without understanding Islam. The basis of their knowledge of Islam is through the materials purposely designed to dismantle unity among the Muslims. The Muslim students hate the orientalist, but they are worshipping their works. They want an ideal Islamic state, but they don't give room for its operation. They are always agitating for the sharia, but they are destroying the moral values of sharia. They are fed by the information revealed by the orientalists, who designed a criminal plot for sowing discord among various sects of Islam, yet there is no important measure which has been taken for its elimination.*[60]

This emphasis has become standard fare in the literature right through the end of the millennium, even in the newspapers. Ibrahim Umar explains, "You only have to be a product of our educational system to know how well our people are brainwashed and programmed to perceive and treat anything that has to do with Islam with contempt, ridicule and terror." [61]

Given their training, those journalists were bound to respond accordingly.

Education in Plateau State has received its share of Muslim ire. *The Pen* writer charges the state with "indirect christianization" in its educational system.

> *For instance, St. Jones Seminary, a purely Christian theological institution, has now been officially affiliated to the Federal Government-owned University of Jos! Degrees, diplomas and certificates awarded by the seminary are now fully recognised by the university. Worse still, pupils and students of Government-owned primary and post-primary institutions are forced to recite Christian verses and scriptures against their will.*

While there are adequate Christian teachers for CRK and Bible studies, there is an average of one Islamic Religious Knowledge (IRK) teacher to every two schools. An IRK teacher attends to a minimum of 150 to 187 students in a particular class and period. Attempts by influential Muslims and Islamic organisations to assist have not been recognised.[62]

We have already learned of *The Pen* accusing the people of Plateau of developing anti-Muslim militarism. The schools are allegedly incorporated in this effort:

> *Normal physical exercises in schools have now been turned into paramilitary training. Muslims have noticed with great concern rampant campings by Christian schools and voluntary organisations where members undergo such training. Students and voluntary organisations now freely use dummy guns or locally-made ones in training.*

It is not only northerners who experience problems with the colonial educational setup. Ansar-Ud-Deen Society of Nigeria, a Muslim organisation in the South-West, published a communique in which it warned against various forms of anti-Muslim discrimination on the part of governments. Insisting on equal treatment for Muslims, the Society demanded that

> *The Federal Government should see to it that all State Governments provide adequate facilities for the study of Arabic and IRK by Muslims in Secondary Schools as well as adequate facilities to enable Muslims in such schools to say the Jumaat Prayers every week during term time. In residential colleges, Muslim students should be provided facilities to say their daily obligatory prayer.*[63]

Before leaving the educational scene, I need to pre-empt a potential misunderstanding. None of the above means that all these protestors against colonial education oppose genuine modern academic, scientific, and technological education. Sir Ahmadu Bello, the Sardauna or Sultan of Sokoto, one of the fathers and architects of the nation, was a great Muslim evangelist and world leader. In 1963, when he was installed as the first Chancellor of ABU, he warned:

> *The needs of modern society are many and varied. It requires specialist, scientific and humanistic knowledge in order to satisfy them, and we must give our men and women necessary education and training in arts, science, engineering, and technology, in order to meet the needs of the society. In a country such as ours, where the number of trained men and women is still small, maximum efficiency and competence is expected of them. These people are the spearhead of our advance into modern nationhood, and it is our duty to keep the spear-point sharp. Let there be no mistake: the challenges of the future will require the highest academic standard of any country in the world.*[64]

This was no obscurantist anti-intellectual perspective. Islam, including revivalist Islam, has high respect for true education. The speech in which the Sardauna was thus quoted was delivered at a conference of northern governors and educationists, mostly Muslims, who were meeting because they were concerned about the poor level of modern education in the northern states. The group included governors who are pushing for the sharia.[65] Clearly, sharia representing a more wholistic version of Islam, and modern education, are not considered mutually exclusive. Many advocates for the one, crusade for the other.

It is not Western or modern education that Muslims oppose, but the colonial-secular version of it. Musa Adebayo, a commissioner in Ondo State and one-time MSS activist, gave a speech at the opening of a Muslim vocational school, criticizing those who emphasize Western education at the expense of its Islamic counterpart. He favoured Western education. After all, the occasion was taking place at such an institution. However, such education "without Islamic morals would only produce half-baked scholars."[66] Similarly, at another educational event in Kaduna, Chief Imam Abdullahi Bichi warned against one-sided education, "since Islamic religion teaches both aspects of education."[67]

Muslims continued to plead for both throughout the 90s. No one less than the Shehu of Borno appealed to the Borno government "to uphold traditional Islamic education" for which Borno was famous, but to "blend it with Western education."[68] Dr. Karima Ahmed Sani, the senior wife of the Zamfara state governor who initiated the drive for sharia by state governments, pledged that vocational and Western education would be provided to take care of the social problem caused by *almajirai* beggars.[69] In a statement on a meeting with Professor Sam Ale, Director of the National Mathematical Centre, Governor Yerima claimed that his administration had from its inception "accorded top priority to education, especially mathematics and science." In fact, the state had "established five well-equipped special science secondary schools," as well as a college of arts and science. In addition, a scholarship scheme had been established for science students.[70] In keeping with this Muslim spirit, an ambitious plan is afoot for the Katsina Islamic Varsity that is expected to open soon with 5,000 students to "promote the teaching of science and the development of the Muslim society in the country."[71]

Abubukar Mujahid, a former follower of El-Zakzaky who eventually separated from the latter in protest over the Shi'ite connection, sees Western education as "a necessary tool." He compared it to a knife that cuts both ways. Technology can both build up and destroy. T.V., for example, can present "uplifting programs for the people." "It's a matter of introducing Islamic values," he declared.[72]

In fact, historically, Islam has been open to education and knowledge from every source, including ancient Greek philosophy. "Islam," R. D. Abubakre asserts, "places great emphasis on acquisition of knowledge. It does not see the store or the dispersion of it as the monopoly of any race or group of people." Learning is exalted "without discrimination against the place or the person from whom it is obtainable." Then he refers to the fact that Islam gratefully absorbed Hellenistic ideas and "adapted Aristotelian philosophy." Thus, though northern Nigerian Islam generally professes great contempt for African Traditional Religion, it acknowledges that historically Islam made grateful use of Greek Pagan philosophy. Even Western education is highly appreciated, but minus its secular component.[73]

ATTACKS ON THE PILGRIMAGE

Another Muslim institution colonialists have sought to destroy is the *hajj* or annual pilgrimage to Mecca, according to Mukhtar Abubakar. The pilgrimage is a strong unifying factor in Islam in that it is the largest and most regular meeting point of Muslims from all over the world. The colonialists have therefore sought to restrict it by carving up the Muslim world into separate nations, all of which require visas and other forms of control. Even after independence, Nigeria still being the "wetbaby"of the UK and the USA, the *hajj* has been subjected to increasingly restrictive legislation. This began during the 1940s with the West African Pilgrimage Agency that was set up "to control, exploit and eventually inhibit the pilgrimage. Today's *hajj* policy has deviated very little from those principles." People used to be free to go on the pilgrimage, working their way across and staying anywhere along the way as long as they liked. This made it possible for even the poor to perform this important rite. However, the restrictions imposed by each nation has made it all but impossible, except to use the official avenues, that is, the controlled and restricted.[74] This article is found in an issue of *The Pen* that emphasizes the difficulties of pilgrims due to neglect, corruption, and bad management on the part of various agencies associated with the pilgrimage, and implies that all those problems are actually part of a continued calculated campaign against the *hajj*. Bad management is not just bad management; defective planes are not merely defective planes. All the problems associated with the *hajj*, all the suffering, they are all part of the effort to undermine and discourage it.

Alleged attempts to undermine the *hajj* continue to plague Muslims. In 1996, Alhaji Abdullahi Aliyu, publicity secretary of the Kaduna State branch of an organisation called Fityanul Islam of Nigeria, publicly appealed to the Federal Government to reduce *hajj* fares, which he described as "outrageous." High fares, he declared, were "a calculated attempt to deny Muslims their fundamental right to worship. He advised the government "to accord religion high priority." His courageous—and also calculated?—defense of the people's interest paid off: He was elected chairman.[75]

Some Muslims tend to look upon the government as the first port of call when there is a problem. The Bauchi State Secretary to the Muslim Pilgrim Board, Alhaji Yusuf Ibrahim, called on the Federal Government to relieve the misery of returning pilgrims whose excess luggage took too long to arrive. The government should make sure that her aviation fleet is up to the challenge and not seek to hand over the responsibility of the *hajj* to private operators.[76]

During Obasanjo's civilian regime, Muslims once again feel threatened. The Federal Government, according to reports, announced its plan "to withdraw its subsidy from *hajj* operations." There was confusion on the issue, since government officials contradicted each other. However, the word of the Muslim Vice President Atiku Abubukar was considered to be the weightier, and his was that the government would retreat from providing full *hajj* services and, instead, provide supervisory functions over private sector bodies who would provide the actual *hajj* services themselves. The idea behind it is that the government take its hands off religious affairs. The pilgrimage re-organisation is simply a natural consequence of that new hands-off policy.[77]

The leader of a rival party gave it a different twist. The decision is not surprising, according to him, considering the Obasanjo government's "past record in denying Nigerians their rights and freedom." He argued that "*hajj* is one of the five pillars of Islam which every responsible Nigerian leader should respect and make easy for Nigerian Muslims who voted him in power."[78] Thus demands for continued government support kept being aired. Alhaji Danlami Mohammed, at the time Executive Secretary of the Plateau State Muslim Pilgrims Welfare Board, "urged" the government "to reconsider its plan to withdraw from the *hajj* operations." This plea, he explained, was necessary because of the importance of this obligation to all Muslims. "I don't think there is anything Muslims all over the country want to enjoy more from the Federal Government [than] assistance for the *hajj*," he said, adding that "it will be completely suicidal to think of not extending a helping hand to Muslims." Apart from its religious obligation, there is the need for "security and other essential services" that make it impossible for the government to withdraw. In addition, when the operation was handled by private agencies, they "were duping innocent pilgrims." Pilgrims became destitute in Saudi Arabia so that the latter's government had to evacuate them, to the shame of Nigeria.[79] Such a vote of confidence in the government is rare and surprising, but when money is at stake...! I have not noticed from the reports that government involvement has made the exercise more efficient. Less surprising to me is the joint call from Muslim Pilgrims' Boards from Oyo, Osun, Ondo and Ekiti states to the Federal Government to decentralize the operation as much as possible by assigning most pilgrim-related functions to various zones. Federal Government should keep its involvement to a bare minimum "to reduce the hardship often experienced by pilgrims."[80]

One M. T. Usman presented a summary history of government involvement in the *hajj*. During the First Republic, that is, the first independent government (1960-1966), the pilgrimage was handled by the regional governments, especially that of the Northern Region, where the Muslims were concentrated. Usman considered that a normal state of affairs. "The mass movement of a large number of citizens over a relatively short period of time necessitated government's involvement to ease such traffic, and ensure safety, welfare, and health." There was nothing "extra-ordinary" here. Other countries, such as the USA and the UK, protect their citizens throughout the world. Even India provides pilgrimage services.

An important change took place, however. Whereas in the earlier years the officials in charge "were assigned for the duration of the *hajj* only, more recently an entire bureaucracy was developed, and permanent departments." Like all others, this is a self-serving bureaucracy, and here comes an interesting clincher: "It is the belief that it is the largesse this *hajj* bureaucracy seems to generate that emboldened their civil-service colleagues to gradually introduce and plant a programme on Christian pilgrimage!" So, the real purpose of the pilgrimage boards is simply to feed the federal and state bureaucracies. Pilgrims largely pay their own way. Government expense is mainly for medical items and consular services and simply to perpetuate the bureaucracy, including such functions as government delegations and the *Amirul Hajj*, the head pilgrim.

There is a difference, however, in the Nigerian *hajj* arrangements. Some other countries generate many more pilgrims than does Nigeria, but their services are smooth and efficient. They never get stuck at Saudi airports for lack of planes, as do Nigerians. The entire procedure in Nigeria is inefficient and corrupt, so that Nigerian pilgrims suffer great indignity every year. It is Usman's contention that all of these problems are deliberate and intentional. The minimal government expenditure on the *hajj* of some 600 million naira only adds to the problem. That sum is "dwarfed by the money spent by some members of the executive on their personal comfort." He concludes that whatever the final decision of the government, the *hajj* problems will not abate until those in charge "throw away greed and resolve to serve their fellow countrymen faithfully, without expectation of personal gain."

WORK-FREE FRIDAY

The issue of work-free days, especially the Muslim Friday versus the Christian Sunday, keeps cropping up. Colonialism introduced the seven-day week with the Sunday as rest day, as well as various Christian holidays such as New Year's Day on January 1. Muslims experience this arrangement as discriminatory. The Muslim Corpers Association of Nigeria called on the government to ensure "fundamental human rights and freedom of worship" in all states so that Muslims can practice their religion "in any state without fear or victimization." Among other things, the "NYSC headquarters should give equal treatment to both Muslims and Christians at the orientation camp by ensuring that all activities stop latest 12:00 noon every Friday to allow Muslim corpers to say their prayers."[81]

Only a few weeks later, M. K. O. Abiola made a similar call for Friday as a work-free day, "so that Muslims can worship just as the Christian brothers do on Sundays." If Christians can have their day, "there is no reason why the same should not be accorded the Muslims," he argued. In addition, he pushed for the first day of the Muslim year to become work-free, just as January 1 is a Christian holiday.[82] It should be realized that even in fully Muslim countries, Friday is not a work-free day. It is not part of the tradition. The call comes up only because of the competition between the two religions.

Nigerian government agencies, who are, after all, largely lackeys to the West and to Christians, are often considered oppressive by Muslims even if these agencies may be headed by Muslims. Ansar-Ud-Deen Society of Nigeria, a Muslim organisation we have met earlier in this chapter, warned against all manner of anti-Muslim discrimination in governments.

> *The subtle discrimination against Muslims by Government Agencies, especially as these are financed by Tax Payers among whom are Muslims. We reiterate that Nigeria belongs to all of us and therefore we should be accorded equal treatment at all times without any prejudice.*

The Friday question was one of the issues addressed:

> *We note with dismay the tendency for State Governments and their agencies in arranging state functions to coincide with the time for* jumat *Prayers, thus negating the fundamental right of the Muslims to practise their religion. Nigeria, we reiterate, belongs to all of us, and it has never happened that state functions are arranged to coincide with Sunday worship in the churches.*[83]

Membership in Organization of Islamic Conference (OIC)

A bitter controversy about Nigeria's membership in OIC arose due to unbelievable clumsy maneuvers on the part of the government. The Federal Government had secretly sought to usher Nigeria into this international Muslim organisation, but the French press announced the move to the world. It started a most acrimonious debate between the two religions. Christians were dead set against it, because they saw it as compromising Nigeria's secularity as well as a further step in the alleged Muslim plot to Islamize Nigeria, while Muslims insisted on its legitimacy and expressed surprise and indignation at such Christian opposition.

Given the obvious economic advantages Nigerian membership would bring, Sheikh Gumi[84] asked why Christians should object to such membership. Other non-Muslim nations—Gabon, Burkina Faso, Chad, Benin, Uganda and Kenya—are members, and profit from it.[85] Apart from such advantages, Christians have no right to object as long as Nigeria has full diplomatic relations with the

Vatican. Why the one and not the other? It has nothing to do with overturning the secular nature of the country, as Christians fear. It is, the Sheikh continued to argue, "unfair to deny Muslims the opportunity to join their fellow Muslims in other countries." Rilwani Lukman, Nigeria's international oil politician, similarly argued that membership would not turn Nigeria into a Muslim country any more than it did to other non-Muslim member countries.[86]

Not surprisingly, the *NN* also editorialized in favour of membership, and argued much like the previous two. Though Christian opposition to such membership is understandable, according to the editor, it is based on the false premise that secularity means "indifference or even hostility to religious values." He favoured both connections, the Vatican as well as OIC. "Those who would rile at either one of the two connections ought to ponder before they allow emotions to get the better of them."[87] Any Muslim-Christian subject touching on the issue of secularism will without fail bring out the emotions and charges of religious oppression from both sides.

Nigerian Muslim and Christians both have a propensity to reduce all issues to that of religious freedom and right. So, too, with the OIC controversy. The Political Bureau, a Federal agency assigned to look into constitutional matters, reported that Muslims argued against the separation of religion and state. Keeping the country out of the OIC would amount to denying Muslims their constitutional rights.

The issue brought the country to the boiling point, so that the Federal Government appointed a panel of prominent politicians "to examine the implications of Nigeria's full membership."[88] Obviously, the government had underestimated the heat this issue would generate. In fact, Karl Maier credits the issue with having set the stage for several years of further clashes.[89] To Muslims, membership was perfectly in order. As far as they were concerned, opposition to it was simply because Christians want nothing to do with Islam and oppose anything that might help Muslims. As long as there is this Muslim connection, Christians will oppose it even if they were to profit from it, while they are blind to their own inconsistency about the Vatican connection. It was a bitter pill for Muslims to swallow when eventually the government of Babangida announced that it would withdraw and Christians had won the day—or had they? Kantiok claims that Babangida's successor, Abacha—and please note that both of these rulers were Muslims—announced in 1998 that Nigeria was a full member.[90]

Years later the arguments still have not abated. Early in 2003, Nigeria's Ambassador to Saudi Arabia, and her representative on the OIC, stated that the "negative perception" of the OIC is due to "lack of understanding of its functions and the advantages inherent in being a member." He argued that "many African countries with predominantly Christian populations are members," including Mozambique, Uganda, Cameroon, Gabon, Ghana, Sierra Leone and Benin Republic. The OIC, he explained, is second only to the UN in terms of members. Furthermore, it is "more Islamic in name than in practice," for "its conferences are devoid of strict Islamic practices." Like "other international conferences, no time is allotted to Muslims to observe their prayers." Some countries even send delegations that include Christians. In the meantime, Nigeria is cheating itself. Since it has delayed to ratify "agreements with the Islamic Development Bank," an arm of OIC, Nigeria is denying itself "the opportunity to obtain interest-free loans."[91]

Degrading Western Female Fashions

In this section I want to cover yet another area in which Muslims feel that colonialism has undermined their religion and which they want to reclaim; namely that of women's fashions. Even in this subject we have not moved far away from concerns with governments, as you will see. This subject can hardly be discussed without simultaneously touching upon the mixing of genders, since that is the context in which dress becomes important. I could have chosen examples from other areas of culture, but this one serves as a good example of how deep and wide the feelings of resentment run.

Since 9/11, Western media have made the world very conscious of this issue. For a while, pictures of and discussions about and by Afghani Muslim women concerning their dress were commonplace, but it is hardly a new concern for Muslims. Throughout the period covered in this study it has been an irritant with Muslims, both men and women. It has provided them with the basis for their claim of obvious superior morality.

All public displays of female sexuality seem to be feared in Islam. Women are expected to do everything they can to avoid constituting a temptation to men. Hence, female fashions are carefully prescribed. The inspiration for this perspective is said to be derived from the Qur'an itself, which reads,

> *Say to the believing women to turn their eyes away (from temptation) and to preserve their chastity: to cover their adornments except such as are normally displayed; to draw their veils over their bosom and not to reveal their finery except to their husbands, their fathers....*[92]

The basic idea is to avoid what Islam regards as "that satanic flood of female liberty and license which threatens to destroy human civilization in the West."[93] The Pakistani writer Maulana Muhammad 'Ali states the general Muslim principle of appropriate feminine dress when the two genders intermingle, something that should be avoided as much as possible. On such occasions, "The Holy Qur'an requires the women to appear in their simplest dress, or to wear an over-garment which should cover their ornaments, at the same time requiring both sexes to lower their gaze." [94]

Turning to the Nigerian situation, the now late but very famous and controversial Sheikh Abubukar Gumi argued that, "women have no business mixing with men and doing men's jobs." It is prohibited. In Mecca, for example, markets are run by men only.[95] "You only find women in places suitable for them." Women should go out only if it is necessary. When they do, "they have to cover all their body."[96] According to Nnanna, the late Gumi spent most of his time exhorting Muslim women to wear the *hijab* and the men to dress according to Islamic law.[97] An equally prominent but more moderate southern Nigerian Muslim, Lateef Adegbite, agrees that whenever women appear in public,

> *they must cover the excitable parts of their body, an injunction which aims at discouraging indecency, but which some have interpreted so strictly that they compel their women to be heavily covered from head to toe...clad in dreary and somber dark apparel.*[98]

Ibrahim Suleiman discusses the issue of Muslim morality in the context of a bid to Islamize Nigerian society as a whole. Such morality would involve "the safeguarding of public morals and the suppression of indecent behaviour, the protection of the honour of the womenfolk and the introduction of modesty in all facets of national life."[99] The protection of that honour includes preventing the mixing of genders. Suleiman is serious, for these statements are a repetition of what he wrote earlier to the government. "It is utterly unacceptable to Islam that the honour of women should be abused...." Abuse here includes the exposure of their bodies or the "public display of immodesty," as well as the "unrestrained intermingling of male and female" as practiced by and imposed on the country by Europeans.[100]

Muhammad Basheer Shomotun describes *hijab* as

> *a simple dress designed by Islam to cover and protect the beauty of a woman regarding her figure and hair. It is a modest mode of dressing which helps to preserve the dignity and personality of women, so that they are not mainly looked upon as objects of beauty and sex.*

They are to be covered entirely, he explains, "with the exception of the hands from the wrist downwards, and the face." Many Muslim women, he laments, have been taken in by so-called modern fashions and ape Western women who see "nothing wrong in moving naked in the streets." Womanhood is reduced "to the level of animalism" and civilization is being destroyed. The *hijab* is a tool "towards purifying society from corruption and all other vices."

He then goes on to complain that Muslim women are *forced* to disobey Allah by wearing indecent Western dress in certain jobs, such as nurses, police women, bank clerks, secretaries, students and members of NYSC. If religious freedom is guaranteed in the country, why should Muslim nurses be prevented from dressing appropriately? After all, Christian nurses are allowed to wear uniforms that conform to their religion. This is a pure case of "victimization" of Muslims and of "deprivation."[101]

One Mu'uza Hardawa wrote a letter in Hausa in *GTFK* that appeared under the heading "He Wants to Prevent Women from Coming to Work Naked."[102] He bitterly complains about the temptations such women put before the men among whom they work. It leads them to the sin of "fornication of the eye."[103] These are not just young girls. Many of them are important women of position dressed in ill-fitting uniforms. Like a good Muslim, Hardawa calls upon the government to put a stop to this kind of shameful attire.[104] On the very next page, one Yusufu I. Abubakar of Katsina writes similarly that the white man's fashions fall short of the demands of the sharia, since "they do not cover the private parts" adequately.[105]

The Chief Imam of a Sokoto mosque, Sheikh Abubukar Jibril, accused the National Youth Service Corps (NYSC), the government service that assigns all graduates to a year of basically unpaid service anywhere in the country, of being "a prime source of the indiscipline for the upcoming generation." The sheikh said, "Mature males and females were being kept in one place "naked" and often asked to wrestle with one another in the name of physical exercise. He said, "How can a healthy man grab a woman in short knickers without nursing any dangerous ideas in his mind?" He "condemned the type of uniform corps members wear and said this was the same with our institutions of learning, especially where there were girls." The sheikh further charged that "the set-up had been deliberately tailored in a way that a first visitor to the country would have the impression that non-Muslims were in the majority."[106]

One Alhaji B. T. Ogunseye expresses the disgust, wonder and amazement Muslims experience when they behold fashion and sexual mores in the West. He describes the situation in strong terms: sexual orgies, debauchery, promiscuity, pornography, licentiousness. "It is incredible and regrettable that modern man...in the so-called developed countries" can engage in all such horrors.

> *This is another wonderful "feat" of the civilised countries, which are not unmindful of the fact that they are inviting Allah's wrath by leading humanity through the blind alley of destruction to annihilation. These "refined people" are conversant with the Bible and the Holy Qur'an. May Allah have mercy on us. Amen.*

This, the Alhaji rightly declares, "is misuse of freedom" and Islam is "vehemently opposed" to it.[107]

Given the Muslim stand on the close relationship between religion and government, it is no surprise that some people are demanding action from their state governments regulating fashions, especially official uniforms. Some governments, in response to such pressures, actually have at one time or another announced plans to take such action. The government of Kano State announced it had designed new uniforms for nurses and nursing students so that these women no longer go about "almost naked."[108]

The National Council of Muslim Youth Organisations (NACOMYO) entered the fray by defending this government action. It observed that "Right-thinking, morally-conscious people have complained against the bad dressing of our women folk, especially with the nursing profession, the police, and serving youth corps members, as their uniforms are too tight and highly exposing." The organisation praised the government for taking action towards modesty.

However, some papers from southern Nigeria,[109] described as "Christian" by NACOMYO, wrote strong articles against any such government move. Their attack is seen as "unjustified criticism" based on "religious parochialism rooted in ignorance." Their "sense of judgment and sensible human reason" is "beclouded." Furthermore, they misrepresent the Christian faith, for the latter "does not support half-nakedness and nudity. That is the reason some Christian churches have their nurses dress in "long gowns, long-sleeved with scarf."[110]

One Alhaji Zubair, an *imam* in Katsina State, and other Muslims, call on the government to ban "indecent dress" among females throughout the country. Sheikh Abubukar Tureta warned Muslims to be on their guard against underground moves to sabotage the Kaduna State Government's intention to stop co-education with its abhorrent gender intermingling. He also advised that the change to the Muslim dress code in schools be sped up.[111]

It does appear that the process of change was slow, for already four years earlier the Kaduna branch of the MSS condemned a group called "Joint Action Committee of Kaduna State Women," for attacking the Muslim dress code approved by the State Government for Muslim female students. The Committee apparently argued that such a move would "dichotomize the students along religious lines."[112]

An article by Alifa further shows us how wide this concern for women fashions has become in Nigeria and that it is hardly a marginal concern. I will let him tell the story:

> *Abuja University sets up a committee on mode of dressing. Worried by the mode of dressing of female students of the University of Abuja, the Vice Chancellor, Dr. Gambo Laraba Abdulahi, has set up a committee to look into the issue. The 11-member committee, headed by Dr. A.U. Okwodishu, was set up to stem what has been described as "unsavoury criticism" from parents and other members of the public.*

A statement from the university noted that the duty of the committee would be to find ways of ensuring decent dressing "for the integrity of womanhood." But the approach would be through pep talks and persuasion. However in a furious reaction, some female students who spoke with *Guardian* frowned at the development, maintaining that the idea was an infringement on their rights. A female student who simply identified herself as Joke said:

> *What rights have they (university authorities) to tell us how to dress? We hope they are not planning to introduce the sharia in the university campus. We are not unaware that the Vice-Chancellor is a Moslem, while about four of the committee members are also Moslems. At least, two of them are known to be fundamentalists in their approach.*

The head of the committee, Dr. Okwodishu, is optimistic that the moral campaign will be successful, because, according to her, some students have already taken the initiative to reward those who dress well. She cited the example of the Education Students Association, which, she said, gave awards to students that dressed well.

Asked if the committee would recommend any punitive action against recalcitrant students, she said she was optimistic of the success of the crusade "because some female students had expressed concern over the same mode of dressing." She also disclosed that a female student was recently slapped by her mother in front of the university library because of her mode of dressing. The mother who visited the university unannounced, according to her, was shocked when she saw the clothes her daughter had on.[113]

In view of the contentious nature of the issue, one could consider it a good thing for the issue to be dealt with. However, the good thing, like so many in Nigeria, was quickly derailed and distorted into a Muslim versus Christian issue. Hence the issue was debated with heat and emotion more than reason. This time the discussion involved not merely Muslim men, but also Christians and women. Out of the eleven committee members, only four or five were Muslims. The question of unbridled freedom came up and of the right to ignore all norms of modesty, a right neither Christians nor Muslims espouse.[114]

The write-up of Daniel has brought us up to the change of millennia. The editor of *New Nigerian* accepted an article by one Muhammad I. Memon in which failure to wear the *hijab* is said to lead straight to hell![115] Now, it would appear, we are reaching the outer fringe of Islam. It is a source of great amazement to me that the editor of a government paper allowed that article!

In this pro-sharia era, in Zamfara State, women are even precluded from various sports because of the sportswear associated with them. It is reported that women are banned from almost all sports, but, apparently, only for the time being. Governor Sani advises that "we should design our sportswear to cover down to our knees as mandated by our religion." Actually, that sounds pretty liberal compared to some Muslim standards. In the meantime, the state allows them to participate in judo and karate since "authorities claim their gears cover all parts of the body, exposing only the face and hands."[116] The state government sought to ease the difficulties some women suffered by distributing the *hijab*, the approved Muslim female dress in public, free of charge.[117]

In 2002 the issue once again heated up to the point of riots, in the context of the Miss Universe contest scheduled to be held in the capital Abuja. Already during the preliminaries held in the southern Nigerian city of Calabar, the home of Miss World 2001, Muslim groups objected to the event as "an abomination and parade of nudity which will promote HIV/AIDS and promiscuity," and threatened to disrupt it. Demands were aired that "the contestants keep off the northern part of the country."[118]

This time the resulting riots received extensive world media coverage, more than any previous riots. All the issues raised in connection with the earlier riots and fashion-related controversies came up again. It became heavily politicized and even came to be regarded as part of the anti-sharia movement. Eventually, of course, the event was moved to London, England. In the meantime, over 200 people were killed, and churches, mosques, and other properties destroyed, in what has become a classic Nigerian tradition.[119]

All the Muslim complaints about colonial and post-colonial imposition of foreign, non-Muslim culture and religion since the aftermath of the 1977 Constitutional Assembly, have remained constant right into the new millennium. They are all related to each other. The aim of the entire enterprise, including all of its various parts, was and remains the destruction of Islam and the imposition of Christo-secularism, an amalgam of two concepts that are mentioned in the same breath and considered synonymous. Fashion is just as much a weapon as are the media, economics and politics. So, it is not so strange for Muhammad Y. Ali-Agan of Bayero University to support the state government's decision to change nurses' uniforms in his article, *Commendable: The New Initiatives in Changing the Nurses Uniforms.*[120] In his article, references to the more general issues far outnumber those to the uniform concern itself, a fact fully understood by his intended readership. I attach the complete article as Appendix 2, for it is so typical of the general attitude, while it summarizes the situation effectively.[121]

In addition to this lengthy prose quote, I treat you to two poems, one in English by Jawayriyya Badamasuyi that is attached as Appendix 3. The other is a Hausa poem, *Rikicin Kafanchan*, by Ibrahim Isa Malumfashi, attached as Appendix 4. The reason for these inclusions is that I want you to *feel* the strong emotions associated with these issues. Even if you are not a Muslim, try to empathize with them and experience their anger and frustration, not to speak of hate and fury. The poem by Badamasuyi is a passionate plea for a return to the simple fashions and life style traditionally associated with the piety and simplicity of Islam, but, ironically, expressed with much hatred, anger, disgust, and contempt—attitudes not usually associated with that traditional piety.[122] The one by Malumfashi expresses Muslim anger about the Kafanchan episode. Both poems express Muslim emotions very well. This Hausa poem is for the benefit of northern Hausa-reading Christians, many of who cannot read this book due to their lack of English. This is one poem they can read.

The issue won't die. As long as I keep writing, so long will riots continue, it appears—and so will the *hijab* issue. In February, 2003, 51 Muslim "fanatics" were arrested in Ibadan for assaulting staff and students in post-primary schools, most of which were founded by Christians. The reason for the assault, according to Alhaji Ibrahim Mukhtar, the Deputy Commissioner of Police for the state, was "to pressure the school authorities to allow Muslim girls wear the *hijab*, head and shoulder cover over the school uniforms."[123]

The Kano State government has made it mandatory for all girls in state schools, regardless of their religion, to wear *hijab*. In 2001, the Bauchi State Government started enforcing Muslim-style uniforms on nurses, since Western uniforms "revealed too much of their legs." Twelve nurses refused to comply and have since been fired. That is now becoming an international issue with the British House of Lords Deputy Speaker, Baroness Caroline Cox, "pledging to use her position and connections to see that the nurses get justice." Christian Solidarity Worldwide is a U.K. based Christian human rights body that is pressing for their reinstatement.[124]

▲ Wrap Up

As we wrap up this chapter, it is plain for all to see that, from the Muslim perspective, colonialism set in motion a process that totally disregarded "independence" as a non-event. Even throughout the post-colonial era, right up till the time of this writing, it nibbles away at the very foundations of Nigerian Islam, all the while draining it of its life sap. The Christo-secular bulldozer seems relentless. Though it is often claimed that the northern vote brought Obasanjo to power,[125] it did not take long for the Muslim northerners to feel that they "had been had." The elite felt that power was slipping out of their hands because of Obasanjo's alleged pro-Christian and pro-south policies. For example, at least a hundred senior army officers were released and then replaced mostly by officers from the Middle Belt and the south. M. D. Yusufu, a member of the northern elite, explained that northern leaders are angry, because they have lost power.[126] You add the anger of the elite to that of the northern peasants, who are suffering from the rising cost of living, and a lack of basic social amenities, and you have a dangerous, explosive, and seething cauldron, the ingredients of which are religious as well as economic and tribal.

Suleiman Kumo, a lawyer said to be a sharia expert, is convinced that the aim of the unholy triad of colonialism, secularism, and Christianity "is to keep the Muslims under perpetual domination."[127] He accuses the leaders of CAN of having no regard for the truth, and of being interested only in "the perpetuation of the domination of the Judeo-Christian world view and philosophy over Nigeria...even though this is against the wishes of the majority." He then directs a salvo against the media, which, together with "their other anti-Muslim cohorts are not even interested in trying to understand the feelings of the Muslim masses on these matters." He warns that "if a group of people allow their rights to be trampled upon for a long time without complaining, they can only get back their rights by asserting themselves," something that may have begun to happen with Zamfara's call for sharia.[128]

Yes, indeed, hatred and anger are prominent components of the Muslim psychological makeup. It is those emotions and that reading of history that undergird the Muslim attitudes towards the riots described in Volume One. Without tying his comments to a specific riot, the editor of *Al-Madinah* warned the Federal Government that the fanaticism that has led to the various riots

> *is the result of systematic, impertinent, and unmitigated provocation. It is generally people who are subjected to quiet, calculated and prolonged religious oppression who burst into huge fire-balls in the end, particularly after all entreaties fail to change the status quo.*

He continued his warning that a fire is not doused by attacking only the smoke. Governments have to pursue the "real causes" of these crises.[129]

Without a strong awareness of all of this emotional turmoil through the course of an entire century against the Nigerian "system," the readiness of Muslims to explode, sometimes at hardly any direct provocation, cannot possibly be understood—or addressed. So, Christian and secular readers, feel and understand along with your Muslim neighbours. Above all, seek ways to address this source of anger and frustration—and replace your anger and hatred with a strong dose of empathy.

▲ Notes

[1] The term used by S. K. Rashid, p. 1.

[2] It almost sounds parallel to the secular dualistic separation of religion and marketplace.

[3] A. A. Gwandu, pp. 10-11 and O. Bello, pp. 28-30, both in Rashid.

[4] *NN*, 21 May/86; 4 Nov/99; 15 Feb/2000, p. 17. *The Pen*, 1 July/88, p. 1.

[5] *NC*, 24 Nov/89. *Guardian*, 26 Feb/88. *NN*, 6 Dec/85, p. 20; 17 Nov/99; 26 Nov/99, p. 5; 30 Jan/2000.

[6] Shaw, pp. 452-453. J. Boer, 1979, pp. 69, 212, 397.

[7] Rashid, pp. 2-3.

[8] *NN*, 5 Jan/2000, p. 14.

[9] Z. Bangash, "*Understanding....*"

[10] *CC*, 4 Sept/98.

[11] Abubakre, p. 64.

[12] I. Bello, 27 Feb/89, p. 13.

[13] Bodansky's book on Bin Laden, a pre-9/11 publication, is replete with such warnings that should have been heeded. It is simply impossible to believe that 9/11 came as a total surprise. All American government claims to that effect must be regarded with deep suspicion. For those who wish to pursue this line, one of several useful resources is the website www.copvcia.com of *The Wilderness Publications*. Bodansky was very courageous in publishing his book, for many people would have regarded him as a redneck, but 9/11 was the fulfillment of his predictions and he moved up from the rank of redneck to that of prophet. Though 9/11 shocked me, it was cushioned by my awareness that something was going to give sooner or later. Even if I had spoken up, who in Washington would have heeded an obscure Canadian missionary in Nigeria if they did not listen to Bodansky?

[14] Hausa original: *"Turawa da suka shigo kasar nan sun yi kokarin lalata duk wata al'ada mai kyau da suka sami Hausawa a kai. Haka nan kuma...a bayan da suka bar kasar nan sun ci gaba da aiko da littafansu da kuma faya-fayan sinima wadanda ke koyar da miyagun dabi'un Turawa a*

kasar nan." *GTFK*, 29 May/99, p. 1.

15 *NS*, 28 Feb/88.

16 *Weekly Trust*, 29 June/2001.

17 *NC*, 15 Oct/86.

18 *NN*, 29 Jan/86.

19 Abubakre, pp. 70-72.

20 M. A. Mabdul, "W.A.I..."

21 Dangogo, 15 July/88, pp. 5, 15.

22 *Jizyar* is a Hausa word for the "poll-tax on conquered non-Muslims," traditionally imposed by Muslim governments. R. C. Abraham, *Dictionary...*, p. 434. If the story is correct, this was obviously insulting the Hausa by treating them as a conquered people or *dhimmi,* and could be interpreted as a class action or revenge against all Muslim governments everywhere for having imposed that tax on non-Muslim religious minorities.

23 Original Hausa: "*Sai ta kore su tana mai kiransu 'Baki' tana kuma tambayarsu cewa yaushe ma suka zo kasar har suka mallaki gonaki da filayen noma?*"

24 *Radiance*, No. 4, p. 16.

25 *NS*, 24 July/86.

26 Under the caption "Ramadan Special," the cartoon in question shows two Muslims bowed down on their prayer mats, while a woman in a minidress walks right past them. One of the men cannot resist the temptation to take the forbidden glance. It is indeed a disgusting, insulting and highly provocative cartoon that should not have been allowed. The original appeared in *NS*, 4 May/88. It is reproduced in *The Pen*, 1 July/88, p. 16.

27 *NS*, 28 Feb/88.

28 *The Pen*, 1 July/88, p. 1.

29 *The Pen*, 1 July/88, pp. 1, 16.

30 *The Pen*, 1 July/88. This has reference to Sunday services in Jos at Good News Church and at the Chicken Market, both about a kilometre from the main mosque, where Muslims started closing major arteries on Fridays years before Christians ever thought of doing so!

[31] M. G. Abdullahi and A. I. Lawal, p. 16.

[32] "Comment: Averting a Holocaust." *The Pen*, 15 July/88, p. 1. Unfortunately, the article is suddenly cut off in the middle of a sentence with no continuation anywhere. There are references to some issues that will come up later in this chapter.

[33] Nigerian Television Authority.

[34] *Al-Madinah*, Nov/95, pp. 3, 4, 10-16.

[35] Again, a parallel to the complaint of many North American Christians about discrimination against them by the secular media.

[36] N. Jalingo, *Weekly Trust*, 8 Mar/2003. It is interesting that in the same issue a *Muslim* complains about discrimination by *Muslim*-controlled public media in the *Muslim* state of Katsina against 30 opposition parties whose local members were mostly *Muslims!* Clearly, Christians have no monopoly on discrimination.

[37] See, for example, A.A. Gwanda in *Rashid*, pp. 10-15.

[38] S. Jahun, *GTFK*, 4 May/89, p. 3. Original Hausa: *"Amma hada kai da sarakunan gargajiya bai dace da hukumar ba. Tun da sarakuna martabarsu ta rushe a idon jama'a to, ba sa jin jama'a za su yarda da fadakarwarsu, domin siyasa ta raba su da jama'a, sai dai hukumar ta yi kokarin dawo musu da martabarsu."*

[39] The original Hausa: *"To, ina jawo hankalinku da cewa duk wanda bai yi aiki da abin da Allah ya fada ba, to, hanyarsa daya sai wuta, sai ko in ya tuba kafin ya mutu. Saboda haka, Sarakuna da shugabanni, a yi adalci, a bai wa mai hakki hakkinsa, ba a tauye masa ba."*

[40] H. A. Gadam, *GTFK*, 7 Oct/86, p. 3.

[41] H. Bobboyi, *The Pen*, 30 Dec/88, p. 5. Bobboyi's punctuation makes it impossible to determine whether Muhammadu Buhari is the author or the recipient of the letter. My decision is somewhat arbitrary.

[42] Bobboyi, *The Pen*, 16 Dec/88, p. 5.

[43] Bobboyi, *The Pen*, 13 Jan/89, p. 5.

[44] B. Isyaku, *The Pen*, 16 Dec/88, p. 10. This was written in the context of the riots in Sokoto about the appointment of an unpopular Sultan.

[45] Comment. *The Pen*, 18 Nov/88, p. 1. *"Sharhin Labarai."* *Alkalami*, 16 Nov/88, pp. 1,3. The materials in this paragraph are taken

from these twin editorials. Reference to Hausa language materials are from *Alkalami*

[46] *Hausa original: "shugaban jama'a ta fuskar siyasa da kuma addini...da kuma yi masu jagora zuwa tafarki madaidaici." "Sarkin Kano da sauran sarakunan Musulunci shi ne karen sharia da ganin kuma al'ummar musulmi ba a taye masu 'yancinsu ba...a takaice dai su daukaka matsayin musulmi da addinin musulunci."*

[47] Hausa original: "*...kowanne sarki ya kamata ya hada kan jama'arsa su gane abubuwanda za su amfane su, sannan su yaki abin da ba zai haifar masu da alheri ba. Yin haka zai kusantar da mai mulki ga jama'arsa, su kara daraja shi, sannan kuma ya sami kyakkyawan sakamako wajen Ubangiji.*"

[48] Hausa original: "*su yi yaki da duk wani abin da ba na musulunci ba, da kiyaya amanar Allah Ubangiji a duniya. Don haka wajibi ne a garesu su yi yaki da danniya da tsarin Turawa da masu neman tilasta wa Musulmi su bi shariar kafirci.*"

[49] Hausa original: "*Takala da wulakanci da kuma tsokanar da ake wa Musulmi abin tuni ya kai matuka.*"

[50] Abdulwahab, *TD*, 14 Nov/02.

[51] Abubakre, p. 64.

[52] In Rashid, pp. 59-61. On these same pages, Suleiman also adduces a quote from Governor Clifford that illustrates how accurately Blyden described the situation.

[53] H. Scott, p. 737. Boer, 1979, pp. 64-65; 1984, p. 16; 1989, pp. 7-8.

[54] Boer, 1989, p. 9. Takaya, pp. 34-35, 51. Balarabe Musa was a civilian governor of Kaduna State, who was deposed precisely because of his challenge to that class. He is the civilian counterpart to Colonel Yohanna Madaki, who was similarly deposed as military governor for taking on the same class in the defunct Gongola State.

[55] Rashid, pp. 69-71. Junaidu's speech was delivered back in 1972, according to A. Dauda, who, 16 years later, reproduces some of the same parts of that speech in his own article in *The Pen*, 1 July/88, p. 12.

[56] Anonymous, *Radiance*, No. 4, pp. 8-11.

[57] Anonymous, *Radiance*, No. 4, p. 30.

[58] A. Dauda, *The Pen*, 1 July/88, p. 12.

[59] A. Dauda, *The Pen*, 15 July/88, p. 11. In this and all other quotes, I take no responsibility for the "imaginative" English and neologisms.

[60] Abdul-Ghaniyy, "*Lesson from....*"

[61] I trust you recognize the humorous inconsistency here? As Muslims analyze the educational system, an average graduate would definitely *not* be aware of the situation described, for nipping such critical attitudes in the bud is alleged to be a major goal. The above article by Umar is basically a report on an interview with Ibrahim Suleiman, a man whom we will meet more frequently in following pages and volumes of this series. He is/was director of the Centre for Islamic and Legal Studies at ABU. He is also member of the Council of Ulama.

[62] *The Pen*, 1 July/88, pp. 1, 16.

[63] Communique, *National Concord*, 17 Apr/88.

[64] A. Abubukar, *New Nigerian*, 13 Feb/2000, p. 19.

[65] See *New Nigerian*, 8 Feb/00, p. 17 and 13 Feb/00, pp. 9, 19-21 for coverage of the conference.

[66] *The Pen*, 13 Jan/89, p. 2.

[67] *The Democrat*, 10 Oct/90.

[68] *New Nigerian*, 28 Dec/99, p. 24.

[69] *New Nigerian*, 9 Feb/00. *Almajirai* are children who attend Qur'anic schools and who are often sent into the streets by their teachers to beg. They often form themselves into bands of hoodlums when riots occur. In some of these schools they are taught hate for and belligerence to the secular establishment, including Christianity, and trained for militant action.

[70] J. Taiwo, *TD*, 13 Nov/2002.

[71] J. Ilelaboye, 22 July/02. His vision is about as audacious as the vision of Abraham Kuyper for the Free Reformed University of Amsterdam where I did my post-graduate work. It had a similar vision for Christianity. Apart from their being based on different religions, two important differences are that Kuyper did not have an opening goal of 5,000 students, and neither did he have the backing of oil rich nations. His financial supporters comprised of his country's peasants and middle class with their pennies and nickles.

[72] K. Maier, p. 171.

[73] Abubukre, pp. 62-63.

[74] M. Abubakar, *The Pen*, 15 July/88.

[75] S. Gaya, 23 Jan/96.

[76] S. Makera, 13 May/99.

[77] Anonymous, *Gaskiya Ta Fi Kwabo*, 30 May/01.

[78] *Weekly Trust*, 16 Nov/2001.

[79] Anonymous, *New Nigerian*, 16 July/2001.

[80] Adele, W., *New Nigerian*, 23 July/2001.

[81] *Nigerian Standard*, 11 Nov/85. "NYSC" stands for "National Youth Service Corps." It is a federal agency administering a program of compulsory national service for tertiary graduates for one year.

[82] *National Concord*, 3 Dec/85. The same call was also made by the National Council of Muslim Youth Organisations as per *National Concord*, 4 Feb/88. Though the demand for work-free Muslim days is heard often, not all Muslims agree as in *Nigerian Standard*, 11 Dec/85.

[83] Communique, *NC*, 17 Apr/88.

[84] Though there is a special section dedicated to the Sheikh below, I have chosen to place this discussion in its present location. Arguments can be made either way.

[85] Gumi's argument here is similar to Abubakre's discussion of Nigeria's failure to attend some major international Muslim conferences in 1974. Nigeria declined sending representatives without so much as an apology, Abubakre complains. Someone must have portrayed Nigeria as "less Islamised than Chad, Gabon, Guinea, Guinea Bisau, Senegal and Uganda." One sad result was that the Nigerian flag did not fly at the Islamic Secretariat in Jeddah, Saudi Arabia. Another sad result was that Nigeria did not share in the investments and tax-free loans the Conference gave to participants. "That," argues Abubakre, "would have saved Nigeria the trouble of having to lobby for loans with interest from the World Bank or International Monetary Fund with its stiff and counterproductive conditions" (p. 71).

[86] *New Nigerian*, 28 Jan/86.

[87] *New Nigerian*, 27 Jan/86.

[88] *New Nigerian*, 29 Jan/86.

[89] K. Maier, p. 65.

[90] Kantiok, pp. 260-261. Check here for further summary of the issue.

[91] "OIC Membership'll Benefit Nigeria—Ambassador." *TC*, 6 Jan/03.

[92] *Qur'an* 24:30.

[93] Donohue, 1982, p. 255.

[94] The Religion...., p. 661.

[95] Even the scholarly Gumi can slip up. He did not know, apparently, that long ago Caliph Omar appointed a female superintendent for the Medina market, according to Ijaz Qamar. Or did he suppress this information as inconvenient?

[96] Zakariya, *Quality*, Oct/87, pp. 34. 36.

[97] Nnanna, *TSM*, 27 Sept/92, p. 10. I suspect this statement to be somewhat of an exaggeration.

[98] Adegbite, 1976, p. 10.

[99] I. Suleiman, 1986, pp. 12-13.

[100] I. Suleiman, 1986, p. 17.

[101] Shomotun, "*Hijab....*"

[102] The original Hausa heading reads "*Yana so a hana mata zuwa aiki tsirara.*"

[103] In Hausa, "*Su suna sanya shi cikin wani hali na zinar ido.*"

[104] *Gaskiya Ta Fi Kwabo,* 1 Mar/90, p. 3.

[105] *Gaskiya Ta Fi Kwabo,* 1 Mar/90, p. 4. In Hausa, "*Ba su da yalwar da za su rufe al'aura.*"

[106] *New Nigerian*, 21 July/86.

[107] I apologize that I have lost this document after this paragraph was written and thus cannot provide the bibliographical data.

[108] *Alkalami*, 20 Jan/89, p. 16. The original Hausa says "*Gwamnati ba za ta amince ta bar matan na tafiya kusan tsirara ba.*"

[109] *Vanguard,* 8 Jan/89. *Nigerian Tribune*, 9 Jan/89. *Sketch*, 15 Jan/89.

[110] *The Pen*, 27 Jan/89, p. 2.

111 *NS*, 7 Sept/93, pp. 10, 16.

112 *The Pen*, 21 Apr/89, p. 16.

113 A. Daniel, *The Guardian*, 27 July/2000.

114 Muslims and other readers may be interested in my detailed comments on these concerns in my *"The Prophet Moses...."* Days 178-205.

115 M. Memon, *"Hijab and the Intention...."*

116 Adewole, "*Weakening....*"

117 L. Abdullahi, "*The True Face....*"

118 A. Ben-Akpan, 11 Nov/02.

119 *CC*, 3 Mar/2003; *TCNN Research Bulletin*, Mar/2003; *Woord en Daad*, Dec/2003.

120 M. Ali-Agan, "*Commendable....*"

121 On the same subject written in the same spirit, see also I.I. Malumfashi, 15 July/88, Appendix 4.

122 Reproduced from *The Pen*, 15 Feb/91, p. 7. I confess that much of it resonates also in my Christian heart against the immodest flaunting by many Christian women of contemporary fashions hardly inspired by piety even on Christian pulpits and other leadership platforms. Apart from the name, the author is not further identified in *The Pen*.

123 R. Yusuf, *TD*, 20 Feb/03.

124 Boer, *CC*. "Islamic Dress Codes on Christian Schoolgirls and Nurses." 17 Nov/2003. R. Ogbonnaya and N. Okon-Ekong, 2 Dec/2003. <www.compassdirect.org>, "British Nigerian Christians Launch Rights Initiative," 15 Dec/2003. Do these Christians understand what they are doing, placing secular concepts of rights above the responsibility for modesty, whether Christian or Muslim? have they ever seen nurses in action as they wear the ugly, degrading uniforms used in Nigeria? *That* style is defended in the name of Christ? Whenever I see these nurses I am embarrassed. Has anger deprived Christians of the capacity to think straight? how far will we allow secularism to corrupt our hearts and minds?

125 Mohammed Ibrahim Hassan, a very prominent northern Muslim politician, claimed that Obasanjo had agreed to an agenda written by the north [S. Ibrahim, 30 Dec/02]. See also M. Ikhariale.

126 K. Maier, pp. 143-144.

127 *New Nigerian*, 8 Nov/99, p. 1.

128 S. Kumo, "*Sharia Is Constitutional*."

129 *Al-Madinah*, p. 7.

▲ THREE

INTERPRETATIONS OF THE RIOTS

▲ Introduction

The point of the previous chapter, I should think, is clear. From the Muslim perspective, the major context of the riots is the colonial imposition of a Christo-secular establishment that has deranged Nigerian Muslim spirituality and institutions. It has created the anger and frustration that mark the Muslim community in Nigeria and that is ever ready to explode at the slightest provocation, sometimes without any at all. However, there are also other reasons Muslims advance that need to be understood, more immediate reasons. I summarize them below under various "causes."

As we turn to examine these other reasons, it will soon become clear that it is hard to separate them, since they are all related to the more remote historical causes and to each other. In fact, a strict separation is an academic exercise that is intended to help achieve greater clarity, but that has no parallel in reality where they are all mixed together.

▲ Muslim Innocence

The first point is a negative one. I begin by noting that there is strong resistance among Muslims against seeing themselves as cause, against accepting any blame or responsibility for riots. They are not the ones to have started the colonial process. Muslims generally think of themselves as either innocent or provoked to such an extent that the provocateur must be held responsible, even if Muslims took the initiative. In addition, there is a strong Muslim insistence that the Muslims are almost always the major victims in terms of death, destruction of properties and imprisonment.

The pro-Muslim magazine, *Citizen*, reflects the general tone. Abdullahi Pindiga from Zaria wrote the following to the editor:

> *In most riots involving the Hausa, the other tribes are the aggressors. They kill and maim the Hausas before the arrival of the security agents. But in most cases, they [security agents] too take sides. They descend on the offended, shooting and arresting them. A commission of inquiry would then be set up to try the rioters, and while the aggressors would go scot-free, the offended are brought to book. This was seen vividly in the Kafanchan riot, which the Hausas did not start but were killed and jailed. During the Sayawa-Hausa Fulani clash in Tafawa Balewa [and] in Zangon Kataf, it was the same story.*[1]

Still in *Citizen*, Jega reports that the Cudjoe Commission investigating the Zangon-Kataf debacle, "laid blame squarely on the Kataf," that is, on the non-Muslims. "The Hausa of Zango did not go beyond the boundary of Zango town during the riots. Furthermore, the evidence...clearly shows that the Hausa acted in self-defence. As such, they suffered most of the casualties."

"Who carried out the killings?"Jega asks. "Many of the Kataf assailants were identified before the Cudjoe panel by the Hausa victims." With such a strong slant, we are not surprised at the editor's reference to "the recent massacre of Hausa-Fulani in Zangon

Kataf."[2] This is the major representative attitude. The only part of this chapter in which there is a more balanced attitude is the one on manipulation.

▲ A Potpourri of Factors

As the above title indicates, I am now turning to a list of factors identified by Muslims to have played a role in the development of Nigeria's explosive climate.

The Incompatibility Factor or Antithesis

One explanation that deserves our attention is the problem of two incompatible systems, or of antithesis. This issue underlies most of Chapter Two and is fully recognized by many Muslim writers, as we have seen, even if the terminology is not used much. The language equating America with Satan is, of course, an expression of a basic antithesis. What greater opposite could a Muslim or, for that matter, a Christian, think of than that between Allah and Satan? The notion was very popular with the publishers of *The Pen* and *Alkalami,* and their pages full of its rhetoric. In Chapter Four we will observe that the same is true for the Islamic Movement that regards the Christo-secular setup in Nigeria as satanic.

In settings of dialogue and diplomacy it is politically incorrect to bring up the subject of incompatibility and antithesis. Abdul-Lateef Adegbite, a moderate leader, had the courage to disregard this "impropriety" at the government-sponsored NIREC conference in June, 2000. The endless sharia crises[3] in Nigeria, he asserted,

> *...are a clear manifestation of the strains of religious pluralism in the country. The two dominant religions...diverge in their respective attitudes to Law. Whereas Islam insists on a religion-based law, modern Christianity appears to reject it. This is why Christians speak of secularity and the Muslims would have nothing of it. This dichotomy, coupled with widespread*

> *ignorance of the status of sharia in Nigeria, has contributed in no small measure to the recent escalation of the sharia crises.*

Adegbite thus recognizes the basic problem as one of incompatibility and antithesis and even suggests that conflict is inevitable: "Where a number of laws and legal systems co-exist, conflicts would necessarily arise."[4]

From the government side, however (even Muslim governments at various levels), this factor does not receive much attention. The reason for this is that it would force governments to look at the underlying hard-core antithetical differences between the two religions, something that could lead to some uncomfortable conclusions. A nation that is trying to forge unity of competing systems is naturally more inclined to emphasize commonalities than basic differences. Such a nation is prone to wishful thinking in hoping that somehow the differences will evaporate without either side having to make important sacrifices.

Even though this factor does not receive much overt attention, I list it as the first in this lineup of major factors, because I believe that its neglect is a gigantic mistake. It prevents Nigeria from taking the bull by the horns, and has condemned her to years of a useless search for so-called "remote and immediate causes" that hardly ever touch the basic problems and therefore never lead to the required fundamental changes. Rather than calling a spade a spade, the preferred way is to let sleeping dogs lie. The problem is, they neither sleep nor lie down. Hence the process of almost unbelievable death and destruction continues undisturbed.

The Misunderstanding Factor

In his quote from above, Adegbite refers to "widespread ignorance" as one of the two major factors, the other being systemic. He is in the very good company of many Muslims both in and out of governments. It is one of the preferred explanations of the more irenic Muslims. It is one of the least painful explanations and does not require any drastic surgery from anyone. All we need to do is to understand each other and things will fall into place. In fact, Muslims often expect that any non-Muslim, once he has been enlightened and come to an understanding of Islam, will surely become Muslim and the problem will have evaporated. That, in fact, was the attitude of Sheikh Gumi who took it to the extreme. The solution to all this is simply for Christians to read both Bible and Qur'an. They will surely become Muslims and we will all be friends![5]

Misunderstanding is dangerous, as Justice Abdulkadir Orire has pointed out. When he was asked to present a paper on the subject, Orire was enthusiastic about the assignment and expected to do "yeoman service to break the barrier of ignorance and misunderstanding." However, he was "taken aback" upon reading some Christian anti-sharia documents from CAN and others.

> *I felt bad and asked myself whether there is any way at all of convincing any Christian colleague in this country of Muslims' good intention about the sharia. There were distortions in these documents about the sharia, deliberately made to confuse anybody...and so create hatred and ill-feelings between Muslims and Christians.*[6]

In situations of dialogue with Christians, both parties often talk about the misunderstanding factor. At a dialogue conference, Yusufu Magaji, Chairman of the Civil Service Commission of Taraba State, emphasized "that the main issue is to reach a stage of mutual understanding and respect for each other's beliefs and way of life." Similarly, Ustaz Farouk Yunus, at the time National General Secretary of the Nigerian Muslim Youth Forum, felt that if Christians understood the reason Muslims demand the expansion of the sharia, they would not treat it as competition. Again, Tijani El-Miskin of the Department of Arabic and Islamic Studies at the University of Maiduguri, "was convinced that if Christians and Muslims really understood their own faith, the problems will be minimized." Enlightened Christians would understand why Muslims cannot accept secular structures, the assumption being that if they did understand, they would accept the Muslim stance. Thus the solution to religious hostility is education of the adherents.[7] In his attempt to prevent clashes in Zaria, the Emir of Zaria appealed to Christians and Muslims to address "their misunderstandings."[8] You do not have to scratch a Muslim leader very much and you will get to the misunderstanding issue.

One question that advocates of the misunderstanding explanation need to face is that of the earlier issue I mention, the systemic or antithetical. Adegbite mentions both in the same breath, as it were. The great importance of mutual understanding is a major premise for this project of mine. I am a firm believer in it. But can it erase the difference, or will it merely help locate the basic problems, as important as that is?

The Religious Factor

A major discussion hinges on the religious factor, though it is denied as often as it is affirmed. Most Nigerian governments, in common with many Muslim leaders, prefer to deny, or at least, play down the religious factor. It is safer. If you deny the religious factor, you are not forced to accuse either or both religions, something that most politicians do not consider politically correct—or that they simply would not dare.

The term "religious aspect" often causes confusion. There is the central spiritual, personal part of religion, the part that emphasizes a person's relationship to God/Allah. It covers areas such as personal devotion to Him, prayer, obedience—in short, the heartfelt part of religion. Then there is the communal aspect, that which refers to the people or *ummah* who adhere to a religion. These two aspects do not always act in concert with each other. It is possible that the communal aspect receives priority over the spiritual. When that happens, the people begin to act like a religious tribe or party that may ignore the personal and even act against it.

In these discussions it is the latter that takes centre stage. The problem is that in the heat of various battles in which religious communities often get caught up, the community begins to take on an interest of its own, quite apart from the spiritual, which it is meant to enhance. The so-called "religious leaders" now have developed vested interests whose relationship to the spiritual becomes increasingly remote. The vested interest of the organisation—CAN, the denomination or the local church; JNI, or the local mosque—or of some of its leaders, becomes the most important focus. The spiritual is forgotten and suppressed. It no longer functions properly. It no longer provides parameters and standards. Religion has now sunk into an abyss of distortions. It has been degraded into a political party or tribe with its own motivations that usually go contrary to the spirit of the religion in question.

In these studies, I will not accuse Christians and Muslims of having totally abandoned the spiritual aspects of their religions. At least for some, those spiritual aspects may still function. They still are deeply devoted to God and want to obey Him and serve their neighbour. However, in the situations studied in these monographs, those spiritual aspects are no longer prominently displayed. I do have the impression that for many main actors, whether people or their organisations, the emphasis has shifted to their own vested interests or that of the organisations. I cannot speak for Muslims, but in most situations where Christians kill, they are no longer guided by Christian spirituality. Anger and resentment have taken over. The characteristics of party or tribe have now become dominant. This is the face of religion that creates so much anti-religious sentiment, but it is a reaction to distorted religion that is now regarded as the real thing. People call for its abolition altogether, and for abandoning God.[9] This is the aspect of religion that is prominent in the current Nigerian struggle. It will be to everyone's advantage to remember this distinction as we go through these studies.

According to Matthew Kukah, under pressure of northern power elite, Babangida, the President of Nigeria at the time, "denied the religious basis of the [Kafanchan] riots."[10] *This Week* features a cartoon showing a military representative of the Federal Government—the President himself perhaps?—denying the religious factor, while the people, dressed in Hausa garb and thus Muslims, double over with laughter while pointing to the foolish speaker.[11] They knew better; they experienced it all on the ground.

Bilkisu Yusuf, an otherwise very clear and hard-hitting writer, succumbed to the same temptation of denying the obvious. She, too, suffered from a reluctance to give the religious factor its due in the Kafanchan riots. After giving a nod to the initial religious impetus in the first phase, and then moving on to the political factor that allegedly dominated the second phase, she asserted that in the third phase, where the riots spread to other cities in the state, neither religion nor politics played a role. At that phase, she asserts,

> *It becomes blurred; you can't see the real tribal or religious thing. In Kafanchan, it started like it was the indigenes against the Hausa-Fulani, but once it spread to these [other] places, the battle seemed to have been directed against Christians and strangers [read: Ibos].*[12]

The conflict in Kafanchan town, the political phase two, was, she admitted, a matter of "indigenes against the Hausa-Fulani," the exact fault line between Traditionalists and Christians versus Muslims. It was a matter of the first two resenting imposed Muslim rule. Once the riot spread to other parts of the state, phase three, by her own admission it became a conflict waged by the Muslim population against Christians. What was so "blurred" about the obvious religious fault lines during those phases? Why the denial, sister Bilkisu? What's up?

The same denial was expressed by the Secretary to the Bauchi State Government, Nadada Umar, in response to a CAN allegation that the most recent chapter of the Tafawa Balewa riot series was caused by the state government's introduction of the sharia. Not only was it a false accusation, but, it was charged, the allegation was designed to incite law-abiding people. A logically curious additional denial was offered by the Secretary: The violence could not have been due to the sharia, for the crisis started on June 15, while the sharia had begun to take effect on June 2.[13] Go figure, someone. Attempts to cover up the obvious are bound to result in creative logic.

Similarly, Danazumi Musa, a member of the 1977 Constitutional Assembly and spokesman for the Hausa-Fulani in Tafawa Balewa, denied that there are/were "religious overtones" in their feud. In response to Osa Director's question during an interview, Musa responded:

> *No religious undertone, because there were Muslims among the Sayawas, even before the jihad. Some have been assimilated into the Hausa-Fulani culture. Though Christians are the majority among them, they try to give it religious undertone, since they hope to get the sympathy of the other tribes and neighbours. The crisis is more political and economic.*[14]

As to the Jos riot in 1994, various Muslim leaders reject the religious interpretation. Sheikh Ismaila Idris, a leader of the Izala group, condemned the riot as unnecessary and unfortunate. Such acts cannot be supported by true believers. The culprits should be punished, he urged. He called on Muslims and others not to be "misled into turning the political problem into a religious one."[15] This last sentiment is typical of the more seemingly irenic Muslim interpretation of such events.[16] The question then is: What is the political factor at work here? We are given no guidance on this score. It is my educated suspicion that the answer would demonstrate a basic religious factor.

Similarly, Sheikh Abdul Yusuf Aziz, secretary to the Plateau State branch of JNI, expressed regret over this riot. His published remarks concentrate on the damage done to the Muslim community, namely the burning of mosques and the killing of a Muslim. Like his Izala counterpart, Idris Aziz feels that the incident had nothing to do with religion. So, he asks in apparent puzzlement, why burn mosques?[17] Unfortunately, he does not tell us what he thinks is the motive. Probably he felt that the events were self-explanatory. And they were—but only to those who have experienced Islam over many years. It almost looks like he took a leaf from Ms. Bilkisu Yusuf's book, but for a Muslim sheikh that might be too much to expect!

For reasons of his own, the activist Sheikh El-Zakzaky was for once on the side of much of the establishment. He declared that the Kaduna episode "is a social problem and had nothing to do with Islam and Christianity." As we have already heard, perhaps *ad nauseam*, "people are frustrated, so much so that at the slightest provocation they become mad."[18] Is their frustration, I ask, not caused by the suppression of Islam and its fallout?

The "nays" do not necessarily have the final word. There are also strong affirmations in the Muslim community of the religious factor. The government of Kaduna State gave mixed signals in response to Kaduna 2000. Governor Makarfi himself expressed his doubt that it was a religious crisis. It seemed to him more a case of "religion being used as a vehicle for destabilising the nation." Whether it makes sense to deny religion as a major cause for the Kaduna riots of 2000 when it was clearly provoked by the sharia controversy, I leave up to you to decide.

Another interpretation also emerged from that same government. It appointed a "Judicial Commission of Inquiry into the *religious* disturbances" in the state. This interpretation is in direct contrast to that of the governor. The notice indicates that this terminology is no mere slip of the pen. For Kaduna, the event is officially dubbed as "religious."[19]

Strong affirmations about the religious cause are found on the pages of *Al-Madinah*. "No other phenomenon has wreaked so much havoc on the Nigerian nation more than religious fanaticism." True, Nigeria has had its share of political and even "football fanaticism," but none have beaten the ignoble record of religious fanaticism. The lanes of [Nigerian] history are littered with corpses of victims of religious crisis in Kafanchan, Maitasine, Zangon-Kataf, etc."[20] No fear of bluntness or political incorrectness here!

The *NN* contains many articles that affirm religion either as *a* cause or *the* major cause of the Kaduna 2000 riots. Abedisi Adekunle and an unnamed colleague are only two examples. Under the caption "Sharia Riots Vicious, Barbaric—House of Reps," Adekunle leaves no doubt as to the religious nature of the fracas. "The House of Representatives has condemned the religious crisis." He also reports that a member, Binta G. Koji, spoke to the House about "the religious violence."[21] An unnamed writer uses the term "religious" generously to describe the riots. He writes of "three days of 'religious' riots." Please note the quotation marks around the term, an interesting twist to which he resorts twice in the article. But he uses the term also without the quotation marks. He uses the term "religious disturbances," the quotation marks being mine this time. The article makes clear the religious nature of the riots also by referring to the close connection with the sharia controversy and to the need for input from both Christians and Muslims. The connection with religion cannot get much closer than that.

In the same issue, on the same pages, another anonymous article relates how the Emir of Zaria, Shehu Idris, prevented the "religious riots" from spreading to his city. He "appealed to both Muslims and Christians to calm down and work out peaceful ways." He expressed the hope that the "perpetrators of the religious crisis" would be brought to justice. He further "commended followers of the two religions for allowing peace to reign."[22] Emirs tend to deny the religious dimension of these riots, but here no such effort seems to have been made. It was all clearly in a religious context. An article in the same issue by Amos Duniya, a Christian, had as caption "N/Assembly to Tackle Religious Clashes," language that the allegedly pro-Muslim *NN* allowed to stand.[23] An Izala scholar from Katsina, Sheikh Yakubu Hassan, discussed the need to punish the perpetrators of the violence of 2000. In the process he freely uses the terms "religious uprising "and "religious crisis." It is all about sharia and that is a religious matter, not politics. Hence, he "implored President Obasanjo and other political leaders to desist from making comments on the sharia issue, because sharia is not a political matter, but the sum total of the life of Muslims as commanded by Allah."

Nevertheless, this emphasis does not prevent him from blaming both government and political manipulators, as we will see under the appropriate headings below.[24]

Shittu Obassa reports that Chief Afolabi, representing President Obasanjo, said that the latter "was deeply touched by the religious riot" and that the government "was aware that the religious disturbance was politically motivated." On the same page, an anonymous staff member referred to the "inter-religious conflict." So, we see a mixture. Ditto for Mustapha Lamidi; though, again, you cannot be sure whether the phrase is the writer's or that of Vice President Atiku Abubukar.[25]

Let us move from Kaduna to another, more recent chapter in the ongoing Tafawa Balewa crisis. Ibrahim Ahmed described the latest Tafawa Balewa crisis as "another genocidal attack on Muslims by their Christian Sayawa neighbours."[26] In the Nigerian context, that amounts to ascribing a basically religious cause to that entire series. So, right up till the end of our period, there were powerful advocates for a religious interpretation. At the same time, in many cases it is difficult to determine whether some of these newspaper references to religion are mere slips of the pen that escaped editorial eyes, or whether this was consciously chosen terminology. It is also often difficult to determine whether these references are the authors' or of the person whose views are being reported. There is an amazing and annoying sloppiness of expression with respect to this very sensitive issue.

The religious factor, combined with a good deal of suspicion, occasionally leads to tense situations. During the last quarter of 2002, I received information from a Nigerian friend that Muslim lecturers in the Religious Studies Department at the University of Jos were accusing the university authorities of planning to eliminate Muslim studies from the curriculum. The "unsubstantiated rumour" led to a "passionate discussion" between Christian and Muslim colleagues, even in this university that, together with its state, was until recently probably the most peaceful one in the north. Indeed, feelings are very touchy and it takes only a rumour to enflame them.

Religious motivations in the Nigerian context sometimes take on very raw and uncouth shape. For example, Mohammad Davou Riyom confessed that, prior to his conversion to Christ, he was "a very proud Secretary of an Islamic organisation called *Jammatu Halkatul Bidia wa Ikamatus Sunaa,*" with its headquarters in Jos. A zealous Muslim evangelist, he "vowed to convert all Christians to Islam and became a great preacher against the Christians. I persecuted Christians and wrote Islamic tracts against Christ." He "preached Islam with great zeal on television and on Islamic crusades. I lived in great affluence and, because of my qualities in spreading Islam, I was dearly loved by other Muslims and received gifts in no small measure."

Continuing his story, he tells how,

> *in the quest for brotherhood in Islam, I used to send Muslim thugs to cause confusion wherever there was a Christian*

> *gathering in and around Jos. I went about condemning them [Christians] and used every available method to persecute the believers.*[27]

Open manipulation, even thugs, were used to cause confusion for a mixture of religious and financial motives.

Then there is the story of Alhaji Dan-Bauchi as he has written it. It is Islam at its rawest. Before his conversion to Christ, Dan-Bauchi, reportedly co-ordinator for all northern activities of JNI, had decided on a programme "to eliminate Christianity." He even set the date of April 24, 1978, to start the campaign. It was to be a campaign of lies and provocation, including impregnation of Christian girls, penetration of Christian institutions, creation of confusion, and publication of provocative literature.[28] It was meant to be an all-out war with no holds barred. The end totally justified every means. Eventually the tables turned on Dan-Bauchi when he converted to Christ and moved over to the receiving end of this hatred.

The last two stories indicate clearly the religious base of much of the turmoil. It may be distorted religion, religion turned into tribe or manipulated religion, but religion it is.

The Political Factor

The next factor under discussion is the political factor. The first need is to discuss some aspects of the relationship between religion and politics. In Islam, these two are never far from each other. Many are the Muslims who identify the two, while attempts to separate them often sound hollow. Chapter Two shows that the identification comes naturally to this wholistic religion. Those who insist on the political aspect as the major motivation for these crises, and deny the religious, seldom spell out the specific political factors. I regard most such explanations as attempts to sweep the real cause under the carpet. *The claim itself is often a political act.*

Political concerns are often based on hidden, deeper and usually unacknowledged religious issues. The 1994 Jos riot centered on a political appointment, the chieftaincy of Jos, that the Muslims wanted to take back. In my estimation, the event was the result of a political attempt to reclaim that chieftaincy, a position of authority to which Muslims, simply by virtue of their being Muslims, the *ummah* of Allah, felt they had a right. It was a position they were once given by the colonialists, but who later took it away from them again to restore it to the indigenes. In spite of their wholesale rejection of things colonial, Muslims did readily accept every power and privilege given to them over non-Muslim peoples and are very loathe to relinquish them even today. It is the same issue that surfaced in Tafawa Balewa and Zangon Kataf. Muslims do not take losing very graciously. Their theology tends towards triumphalism and only allows for victories. It was that hidden theology, or, perhaps a better term, religious world view, that in my estimation constituted the basic motivation of the Jos episode. Political reality had to be brought into line with a deep, often unspoken, largely unconscious, religious world view of power and domination. Echoing Chapter One of this volume, Akbar Ahmed states in his video that "in Islam religion and politics are one." This stance is often just below so-called political issues. Though those two Muslim leaders in Jos denied the religious factor, it was there, below the surface. They may or may not have been aware of it. It depends on their awareness of their own world view.

They may also have denied the religious factor for a consciously political reason, namely to avoid blaming Muslims—or would this be a religious reason? Being religious leaders, it was in their interest not to see their beloved religion blamed. So, politics is always a ready scapegoat—as long as no one asks for too many details. But that their denial was shaky was clear from the fact that religious buildings were attacked. Though he regarded it as a political event, Aziz asked with an incredible and feigned attempt at surprise, why then the burning of mosques? Yes, indeed! Without apparently realizing it, he let the real cat out of the bag!

Akbar Ahmed may have an explanation for that. In his video coverage of the 1982 Kano riot, he explains that this and other incidents of violence are not anti-Christian so much as against the entire secular system. "Unfortunately," he explains with a face that exudes innocence and hurt, churches are the only visible representations of that hated system and so Muslims naturally turn on them! What, I must ask, of the omnipresence of buildings that belong to the hated secular government, both state and federal, throughout Kano state? They are the most visible and most readily available presence of the secular enemy, much more so than churches. They should have been attacked, according to his reasoning.[29] Churches in Kano State are few in comparison. Ahmed's presentation is based on the suppression of some crucial facts that renders its validity doubtful.

Even when riots are obviously inspired by sharia issues, some diehards will insist on a political motivation. Obed Awowede reports just that about the Kaduna 2000 riots. "Competent sources," he writes, "insist that the Kaduna crisis was beyond religion. It is not religion. It is politics."[30] No further explanation. Of course, if the sharia issue itself is seen as a political rather than religious issue, then the riots about the sharia could also be regarded as political, but that subject is reserved for a future volume.

This paragraph is being written during the United Nations' debate about the US-Iraq crisis. The Minister for Nigeria's Federal Capital Territory, Alhaji Mohammed Abba-Gana, feared the rise of violence in his area. As a pre-emptive measure, at a meeting with religious leaders he insisted that the problem between the two countries "was not religious and should not be seen as an avenue for another religious riot." Both countries are pursuing their own interests, he asserted. People should not misinterpret it as religious.[31] The motive for the denial is clear. In Nigeria it can be dangerous to interpret events religiously.

As pointed out in the previous paragraphs, it is almost impossible to separate the religious and political in Islam. However, for apologetic reasons, some Muslims have separated them in the context of these riots. So, it needs to be covered under its own separate heading. However, remember that throughout this discussion we are never far from religious motivations.

The political factor has various angles, only a few of which we will explore. Some of these again overlap with each other, or with economic and sociological issues. Those we will refer to include the following issues: government partiality, internal colonialism and indigenousness, lack of appropriate government action and the manipulation factor.

1. Government Partiality

Neither Muslims nor Christians ever tire of accusing the Federal Government and some state governments of being biased in favour of the other. It is perceived everywhere, no matter what the government does or does not. If Muslims do not make the accusation, Christians will. Sometimes both make the accusation for the same situation!

This perception played a major role in the Bonnke riot in Kano. We have already heard in Volume One that, while the government had refused visas to some world famous, popular Muslims, Louis Farrakhan and Ahmed Deedat, of the USA and South Africa respectively, the Christian evangelist Bonnke was allowed to come and hold his revival. This perceived government partiality led to Muslim anger. In that tense context, Christians had the bad taste of aggressively promoting Bonnke with loudspeakers in Muslim neighbourhoods. It was a riot almost engineered to happen by the government and Christians. Hence Nuuman Habib, editor of *Triumph,* declared that the "blame for the crisis fell squarely on the shoulders of the Christians and [the] regime."[32]

Of course, having basically defined Nigerian governments, their institutions and agencies in terms of the Christo-secular-colonial heritage, Nigerian Muslims would expect partiality towards Christians. Ustaz Salihu experienced it personally and routinely as President of MSS at the University of Jos in matters such as "timetable palaver, poster removal, desecration of the Holy Qur'an, and bus preaching." Then there are the larger national issues earlier identified such as "national weekend, school uniforms, OIC, National Pilgrims Commission etc." In all of these, Christians allegedly have the upper hand. Yet they "continue to cry wolf, always alleging government favouritism to Muslims. These are sore points that need discussing honestly."[33]

2. Internal Colonialism and Indigenousness

Then there is Bilkisu Yusuf, at the time editor of a Kano-based Muslim paper. Though, as already seen, she recognized that the Kafanchan riots "started from religious conflict," she felt that "other factors must have been responsible for such an explosion." Amongst these the political is a major one.

Specifically, the political issue Yusuf recognized is the *resentment of the indigenous people about being under the Muslim Emir of Zazzau or Zaria.* Like similar arrangements in Tafawa Balewa, this one was imposed on them by the colonialists. It is usually a matter of a Muslim ruler imposed upon Traditionalists, who, after many of their people turn Christian, begin to wake up to the nature of this internal colonialism, resent it and begin to struggle against it. In the case of Southern Zaria, the area in which Kafanchan and Zangon Kataf are located, an important early stimulant to the push for liberation from the imposed Muslim regime was the doctoral dissertation of Yusufu Turaki at the University of Boston, United States. It is this resentment that led to the explosion in Kafanchan town, after it had begun at the college for religious reasons.

Five years later, Bilkisu Yusuf is now editor of *Citizen* magazine. She wrote an interesting column in which she coined a new term: "katafisation of mankind." She displayed little sympathy for the Kataf people. While she gave some credence to the "emir problem" in the case of Kafanchan, five years later she had little sympathy for it with reference to the Kataf. She wondered whether they had an "intrinsic trait that makes genocide an acceptable method of expressing grievances." She accused people like Yohanna Madaki, a colonel dismissed from the army for his challenge to the Muslim establishment in Muri during his tenure as Governor of Gongola State, of contributing to the troubles, with talk of Hausa-Fulani domination. In an interview he granted, he alleged that "the largely Christian Kataf never had anything to do with either the emirate of Zazzau or the Sokoto Caliphate under whom the Kataf are now subjugated."[34] Yusuf gave a historical rebuttal to these claims that appears below, after the materials on Bauchi.

In reflecting on the first riots in Tafawa Balewa four years earlier, the Military Administrator of Bauchi State, Rasheed Raji, during a 1995 interview with *Newswatch*, declared that "by God's grace, the old wounds have been healed. People are moving about without much problem." He admitted that there were continuing clashes. Though the promised chieftaincy had not yet been established, "it can be created anytime," he purred. At least, the administrator admitted to the basic long-standing problem regarding chieftaincy: "These are problems that have been on for years, since 1916." It is highly unusual for both government officials and Muslims to admit this chieftaincy problem. It was an unusual venture into political incorrectness.

When asked about the number of people killed in this fracas, Raji was more honest than most government officials and Muslims, though hardly generous.

> *They were killed. Why do you need to refer to that? Think about development, and forget about those who were killed.*

> *You see, during crises there is no how there will be no casualties. It is very unfortunate to the party that is affected. The only thing now is for us to pray that God should forbid the occurrence of such crises in future. If I should go by the number of people killed, the old wounds will now resurface and from there people will begin to think about it again. So, it is better for us to forget it.*[35]

And what of the reports of the two committees assigned to study the upheaval? The answer here also bears repetition:

> *What we did when I got there was to review the report from the two committees. There was a panel and another committee on the same issue. But you see, they did not actually address the issue of implementation. They were all coming out with recommendations. But how do you implement it? So we reviewed the issue; made recommendations to the federal government. After a while, we sent a reminder that we were still waiting for these our recommendations to be approved.*

You, the reader, can think of your own terms for such evasions.

Turning to the second installment of the Bauchi riots, we find Danazumi Musa strongly rejecting the religious explanation in favour of the political. His perspective represents a stark opposite to that of Baba Peter Gonto, a representative leader of the Sayawa Christians, whose perspective is described in Volume Three. You really need to read both perspectives next to each other to appreciate the difference. Without doing detailed research into the local history, one has no basis for choosing between the two opposite versions, except to indicate that the differences have to do with the distinction between the town and the local government area. While Gonto in Volume Three speaks inclusively of both town and district as one entity, Musa speaks exclusively and emphasizes the distinction, with the Sayawas being rural dwellers and the various

Muslim groups urban. I attach Musa's explanation, minus the section quoted above, as Appendix 5. It is not the first time vested interest has influenced "objective" thinking!

The Sayawa, according to Musa, had no presence in the town until very recently. They lived in the villages. However, Gonto, their primary politician, riled up the population by beginning a demand for an indigenous chief of Sayawa background. His goals included taking over power in the town. Since he had no historical or present justification for such a goal, his people never having lived in the city, he used political trickery and deceit. Please read Appendix 5 for the full story.

Astounding as the differences between the stories of Musa and Gonto may be, Musa's arguments are not unique. You will come across them throughout this volume. With apologies to the Muslim community, I must explain that he represents what seems to non-Muslims the classic haughty Hausa-Fulani-Muslim attitude towards people of Traditionalist background. They are often considered deceitful, not enterprising, jealous and irrational. Of course, the Christian counter-arguments found in Volume Three are no less classic.

Not all governments accept such "remote" historical causes as explanations for some riots. The largely Muslim Kaduna government rejected such issues advanced by Christians as causes of the Kafanchan riots. At the same time, the Donli committee did accept similar remote causes from the Muslim perspective. But then, vested interests have been known to override logic before. Kukah, always to be counted on for tasty morsels at just the right time, tells us that the issue of chieftaincy in Southern Zaria goes back to 1967. At that time, the emir stated that this attitude would lead to "the people of Southern Zaria to one day demand their own district officers, their own province, and then resident and then a state of their own and chiefs."[36] Apart from its rejection of the apparently hallowed designation "Southern Zaria," the Kaduna government was faithful to a long tradition. In response to the Donli Committee's suggestion that the chieftaincy issue be considered, it said that it saw no need for change in this regard. "The case of Jama'a [Kafanchan] does not warrant any need for change in the selection procedures of the traditional ruler at this time."[37]

The questions of the imposition of Muslim emirs and that of indigenes cannot be separated. The Kataf claim that they are the original inhabitants of their area and that the Hausa-Fulani are merely settlers who subsequently have wrested control from the locals. Yusuf appeals to the writings of Michael Crowther and Bala Usman, British and Nigerian historians of repute, who, she alleges, both show that Kataf land, together with Southern Zaria in general, were part of the emirate of Zazzau [Zaria]since the 15th century and that Islam was there prior to the 19th century Fulani *jihad*. In addition, Bala Usman, a Muslim academic who has long waged war against what he regards as an oppressive Muslim oligarchy in the north, argues that the question of indigenousness is very confusing, since there are some 50 nationalities in the area. Who, then, Yusuf asked, is an indigene? Can a people who have been there for over 300 years still be considered mere settlers without a claim?[38]

In the same issue of *Citizen*, Mahmud Jega also tried to set the historical record straight with respect to the Kataf, but his story does end up with their demand for their independence from the Emir of Zaria. As he tells it, "While the Kataf see the whole district, created in 1914, as their land, they concede that the Hausa arrived there in 1650 under the leadership of one Mele, whom they allowed to settle." Some time later, the "Zaria emirate took Kataf land into its fold and for many decades sent Hausa chiefs from Zaria to rule the district." In 1967, Bala Dauke Gora, a Kataf Christian, was appointed to a minor chieftaincy and as district head of Zango. "This concession has only slightly appeased the Kataf, who now want a chiefdom of their own independent of Zazzau" or Zaria.[39]

Matthew Kukah asked one Alhaji Nuhu Bamali about the cause of the Kafanchan riots. The Alhaji identified the same political issue as the major cause. He blamed the university graduates from the area for setting their parents against "us" by "causing confusion with all this talk about slavery.... We all used to live happily as one family."[40] The students to which Bamali referred are mostly Christian. They are now blamed for no longer accepting the "happy" situation during their days of ignorance. Yeah, right! Happy for whom?

There is an interesting tidbit of history that may help answer the question. Kukah tells us the story of Emir Ja'afaru of Zaria, who in the 1950s had said that "non-Muslims were meant to feed and sustain the power quest of the ruling class." He drew a parallel to the horse and the grass and warned that "the grass must never be allowed to eat up the horse."[41] And then there is still the land issue, part and parcel of the indigene question. According to Jega:

> *The Kataf resent a 1920 edict by the then district head Ja'afaru, later the emir of Zazzau, that appropriated all farmland within a four kilometre radius around Zango and declared it hurumi, that is, land directly controlled by the emir of Zazzau. The Kataf now claim that the hurumi took over their farmland, but no evidence of such appropriation was tendered before the Cudjoe panel. The Kataf demand that this land, now largely owned by Hausa farmers, be returned to them, was disavowed before the commission....*

It appears that the disavowal was due to the fact that the Kataf did not make their claims within the legal time limits.[42]

I find it very gratifying that during the election campaign of 2003 a number of very prominent Muslim politicians have come around to supporting the campaign for a separate Southern Kaduna state. Former Head of State, Babangida, and the Speaker of the Federal House of Representatives, Alhaji Ghali Umar

Na'Abba, among them, along with Governor Makarfi of Kaduna, all have come out in favour. Babangida was even the chairman of a major public campaign in Kaduna to raise funds for that purpose. Agitation for this separate state, he declared, "was most appropriate as it was right for people to seek self-determination." Makarfi promised the support of his government for the quest.[43] At least on the surface, it appears that the agitation of years finally is beginning to pay off—but at a very high cost of thousands of lives and innumerable properties.

3. Lack of Appropriate Action by Government

Yet another political issue is the alleged *lack of appropriate action on the part of the government* in addressing the underlying problems that caused the riots, in stopping them, and in punishing the perpetrators. The police appear almost without exception in the worst of lights for either showing up too late or for being part of the problem, not infrequently complicating situations. Everywhere in the literature from both Muslim and Christian authors the same complaint is aired, namely that succeeding governments fail to take appropriate action in response to riots. It can be weak action, wrong action, or no action at all. The problem with such failure is that it encourages the next dissatisfied group to similarly resort to violence. This becomes even worse when the government rewards the community for their riotous behaviour. To top this off with partiality and alleged one-sided punishment of the Muslims, who are merely the innocent victims, while the guilty parties go free; well, we end up with situations that are simply intolerable and explosive.

The Bachama story as told by Muslim Hausa-Fulani settlers appears to be a perfect example of all of these problems. The issue was land claimed by both. The Bachama claimed it as theirs, while the settlers of half a century alleged they were given it legally and then developed it from scratch. When the latter sought government protection against raiding and killings on the part of the Bachama, every level of government failed to take responsibility. They all were partial against the Hausa-Fulani. All the victims were Hausa-Fulani. Months after the conflagration, the government had still not published the report that a committee was assigned to create.

Lawal Yusufu Mohammed of Bauchi, in a letter to the editor, aired his strong grievance as follows:

> *In 1987, Muslims were massacred in Kafanchan, and when their brothers reacted in parts of Kaduna State, they were arrested and jailed. No single Christian was arrested there. In 1991, Muslims were murdered in Tafawa Balewa; and their brothers who reacted in Bauchi were massacred by security agents, many in their own bedrooms. No single Basayi was arrested. Instead, they were rewarded with a chiefdom. Any wonder then that the Katafs attempted to annihilate the Muslims in their midst so that they too can get their own chiefdom?*[44]

Please remember the 1995 interview by *Newswatch* with the then Governor Rasheed Raji of Bauchi. The first reference to this interview was to indicate that at least for once the underlying problem was admitted by a governor, something that seldom happens. This second reference is to point to the lack of action by the government about a problem that was acknowledged to have existed since 1916! The governor was asked about the reports of the two committees assigned to study the upheaval. His answer is a fine example of failure to act, and buck passing. He replied, and I repeat his answer for your convenience:

> *What we did when I got there was to review the report from the two committees. There was a panel and another committee on the same issue. But you see, they did not actually address the issue of implementation. They were all coming out with recommendations. But how do you implement it? So we*

> *reviewed the issue and made recommendations to the federal government. After a while, we sent a reminder that we were still waiting for these our recommendations to be approved.*[45]

Any need for comments?

The Cudjoe panel dealing with the Zangon-Kataf episode was dominated by Muslims. It castigated the Kaduna government for

> *lack of decisive and prompt action by various governments in the state to defuse tension in Zango and other places. The Kaduna State government is yet to implement some of the aspects of its white paper on the report of the panel that investigated the 1987 Kafanchan riots.*[46]

It is really a dreary and shameful refrain—and it continues to be sung.

With respect to Kaduna 2000, Umar Sanda wrote that "the capability of the law enforcement and security agencies in detecting and nipping in the bud unlawful activities is seriously called to question by their performance." As to the government itself, he did not beat around the bush: "The spate of violent communal and religious crises in the country the last few decades is symptomatic of one problem: the failure of the state. It is high time the state performed its reason for being. It is high time government governed."[47]

The stories and accusations are many, far more than can possibly be recorded here.

Nigerian governments sometimes try to give the impression of being in control and of intending to take drastic action after riots have occurred. After the Kafanchan episode, President Abacha spoke toughly to the nation. He ordered the establishment of various investigative bodies at federal and state levels. He banned religious organisations from all institutions of higher education. He assured the nation the government would "not recognise any sacred cow and none will be spared. Enough is enough." Nigerians, according to Kukah, had high hopes for some tough action this time, but, as usual, it just fizzled out through delay and inaction[48]—but that is for our next volume, since his is a Christian opinion. The President's statement "Enough is enough" continued to haunt the government. Christians have not allowed it to be forgotten.

Muslim complaints in this area are nearly universal. There are, for example, the scathing comments by Muslim scholar Sheikh Yakubu Hassan, an Izala leader from Katsina. Addressing a news conference in Katsina, the Sheikh blamed the Kaduna 2000 uprisings on the "non-punishment of culprits of past riots in the state." He argued that "perpetrators of the Kaduna riots embarked on the mayhem because those who participated in the previous crises in Kafanchan and Zangon-Kataf virtually went scot free." He predicted that "unless the government fished out and punished the culprits, there will be no end to religious crises in Kaduna, as the arsonists will continue to be encouraged by government's inaction."[49]

It is discouraging how the same demands on, and the same promises by the government continue to be made, riot after riot. However, after the riot over the Miss World contest in Kaduna in November, 2002,[50] Governor Makarfi promised that the state would "leave no stone unturned in bringing the culprits to book." He continued, "Those who will be involved shall be punished according to the law. We are left with no option but to take a very much more decisive action against perpetrators of crisis and the dastardly acts." Another "high" government source was quoted as saying that "the state government had resolved to punish the masterminds to serve as good precedence in checking any future reoccurrence"—all are most familiar promises heard after every riot. At the time of writing, it is too early to predict just what will really happen, but at least "about 1,000 persons arrested by the police in the thick of the four-day violence that devastated Kaduna last week, are to be arraigned in court today." In addition, in Abuja, about 100 persons were arrested in connection with the spill-over riot that took place in the Federal Capital Territory. That was unusually quick action. The Governor promised even more: "We must all fight these people through a resistance to violence. And the authorities have been fully mandated to take punitive measures to deal with the situation. Also, all those arrested for murder, theft, and arson will be charged to court on Monday," he disclosed. "We shall deal with individuals as they were caught committing any offence, and such shall be done no matter how highly placed the individual may be." At least, a familiar sound!

A significant development is that during the weekend soldiers arrested the Secretary General of Supreme Council for Sharia in Nigeria (SCSN), Malam Nafiu Baba-Ahmed, for alleged complicity in the riot.[51] This was not a "small fry" catch. It evoked immediate Muslim reaction. The Malam's lawyer, Alhaji Ibrahim Umar, expressed fears that the development might engender fresh protests. "It is lamentable and sad to hear that the Secretary General, Supreme Council for Sharia in Nigeria (SCSN), was molested and arrested yesterday, around 9:00 p.m. at his residence, by some military personnel, and taken to an unknown destination."

He further said that the "unconditional release of Malam Baba-Ahmed is a pre-requisite condition for peace in Nigeria." With the Muslim governor arresting such a prominent fellow Muslim, I am somewhat optimistic that earlier lessons are finally taking hold and that this time there will indeed be no "holy cows." As to the lawyer's demand, what else are lawyers for?

Perhaps this unusually aggressive action was due partially to international attention this riot gained. It may also be an attempt to pre-empt the "Northern youth group, Civil Rights Congress (CRC)" that,

> *has pledged to assist the Federal Government expose the sponsors of the recent violent protests in Kaduna, even as they canvassed capital punishment for those convicted. Its president, Malam Shehu Sani, who spoke in Kaduna yesterday, hinted that the group had resolved to set up an independent investi-*

> *gation team to trace those who sponsored the riots. He said it would make its report known to the Federal Government so that the people behind it would be brought to book. Sani, therefore, called for capital punishment on individuals or group leaders behind the incident. The northern youth leader said that the mandate of the committee was first to go the suburbs and find out who killed and who was responsible for the killing of who.*
>
> *"We also want to find out the extent of involvement of groups and highly-placed individuals within religious circles that are involved in this massacre and we also want to know the level of involvement of security agencies, and why they were so relaxed until the protest that started the crisis got out of hand," he added. He expressed the group's dissatisfaction with the manner in which the state government was handling the violence, stressing that "each time there is crisis in Kaduna, people have always been arrested and released later.*
>
> *"And sometimes, most of those arrested are not really the people on the ground when the offence was committed, and the people behind the riots are not normally arrested. But this time around, we have resolved to expose them and recommend them for severe punishment by the Federal Government," he stated.*[52]

This stance may have seemed threatening to the government and even brave. However, a year later, by January, 2004, I have not heard about any report of their findings nor of any action taken. It appears this private venture ended like its government counterpart: never published and the threatened action never taken.

It is, of course, never good enough. Though, compared to earlier incidents, the government reacted fairly quickly, the CRC not only declared that they "unambiguously condemn the resort to violence that has brought about lawlessness and disorder," but its

Secretary General, Malam Nasiru Abbas, observed that "the steps taken by the government and security agents were too belated. If action were taken earlier, many lives could have been saved."[53]

I reported earlier on the perceived negative and inadequate role of the police in many riots. Other security bodies generated similar negative reports. On the whole, the army appears much better in the course of various riots than the other security forces, at least in the non-Muslim press. The army often has come in when the other security agencies were clearly unable or unwilling to handle the situation. But sometimes even they seemed involved in negative ways. I am hesitatingly wondering whether this situation is increasing under the Obasanjo regime. The Tiv people of Zaki Biam, Benue State, can testify even about an army gone amuck by gunning down hundreds of people early in the new century. Christian women, after the Miss World debacle in Kaduna during 2002, likewise asked about uniformed soldiers attacking innocent civilians. They are not the only ones.

The major Muslim complaint about all security forces, including the army, is that they are pro-Christian. The Council of Ulama accused the army of waging war against Muslims

> *to defend Christianity and persecute the Muslims. The army is the crusader force that is the sworn enemy of Islam. The State Security Services (SSS) are also at war with Islam, at the insistence of a Christian clique with which they have entered into a conspiracy to undermine the Muslim community. Muslims are in the majority. There is no reason for the imposition of Christian governors over Muslims. Muslims will not accept a situation whereby the nation's armed forces, the Police and the SSS are turned into bastions of Christianity, which can be marshalled out against Islam. Muslims all over the country are called upon to take all necessary steps to defend themselves, as they can no longer rely on the state security agencies.*[54]

These were no mere afterthoughts. They were repeated in other contexts. In a statement to the Karibi-Whyte Tribunal, appointed to investigate the Kafanchan ruckus, the Ulama wrote that

> *the army let loose a reign of terror on the innocent and defenseless Muslims and made indiscriminate arrests in Katsina, Kaduna, Zaria and other places where more than one hundred thousand Muslims are now in army cells, with many of them including women and children.*[55]

An ordinary Muslim in Kaduna, Mohammed Awal, caught in the Miss World mayhem of 2002, charged,

> *Our security agents actually contributed a lot. Instead of them defending the interests of the community, they were one-sided. So we are using this opportunity to call upon the federal government. Let them be sincere in a situation like this, let them give us justice, and not take a side.*

His charge is supported by Dr. Abdulrahman Suleiman, a medical doctor in a hospital where many Miss World victims were receiving treatment. Of the 200 victims his hospital treated, 180 came for gunshot treatment. Most of them claimed they were shot by soldiers, he reported.[56]

Lack of appropriate or simply inappropriate government action has also long been recognized with respect to government appointments. A typical instance was noted just before this book went to press. The SCSN requested that the recently re-elected President Obasanjo review the list of appointments he had made to the Federal Executive Council. Muslims are under-represented, according to them. JNI demanded "an explanation for the appointment of 42 ministers out of which only 16 are Muslims." Ibrahim D. Ahmed, SCSN President, declared at a press conference that these and other appointments were "deliberately skewed to favour Christians." There was, for example, not a single southern Muslim amongst them. Then there is the issue of advisers. "In Obasanjo's appointment of Special Advisers, out of a total of sixty, forty-seven (or seventy-eight per cent) are Christians, while a mere thirteen (or twenty-two per cent) are Muslims." This situation "defies logic" and "is in complete disregard to the religious make-up of Nigeria and its laws." Ahmed then slipped in another issue as well. He wants "authorities at the Nigeria Defence Academy to reverse the decision to abolish the study of Arabic language at the institution." The reason for this demand is "Arabic has been in this country for centuries and it is the lingua franca of about eighty million Muslims, and the official language of at least seven members of the African Union, and at least ten members of OPEC."[57]

Complaints about representative appointments go back many years on both sides of the fence. Both claim to be under-represented! The basis of these claims is always the census, with both sides claiming majority status. The games go on....

4. The Manipulation Factor

Manipulation is often said to be a major factor in Nigerian riots: manipulation of religion, usually on behalf of religious, political, class, and other vested interests. It is really just another name for a certain style of politics. It could be argued that it is Nigeria's major political style. Yahaya Kwande, a former Nigerian ambassador and convert from Christianity to Islam, affirmed that religious conflicts are provoked just for such reasons.[58] L. J. Isa, at the time Kaduna State Military Administrator, also stated that people fomenting religious crises are doing so for their own selfish interests.[59] That is the short of it, with the longer following herewith.

Yusufu Bala Usman, a former history professor at ABU, has given us a working definition of manipulation that will underlie the discussion on the subject. It means "controlling the action of a person or group without that person or group knowing the goals, purpose and method of that control and without even being aware that a form of control is being exercised on them at all."[60]

The Potiskum riot is an example of Muslim manipulation of other Muslims in order to get at Christians. The pretext for this riot was the claim by Muslims that a nineteen-year old Christian girl wanted to convert to Islam but was prevented by her parents and the police. One official report asserted that this issue was used as a pretext for "political machinations by the Bolewa ethnic group in active collaboration with the Hausa-Fulani ethnic groups in Potiskum." The state's Police Commissioner claimed that the incident was a case of "manipulation of the Islamic religion for political purposes" in the interest of "the feudal emirate institution. Islam has become a ready tool to suppress the other ethnic groups." He blamed the crisis on the Vice-Chairman of the Local Government, Yusufu Umar Kukuri, who "mobilised the fanatics to carry out the mayhem." His goal was to eliminate "prominent Kare-Kare personalities, who are Christians."[61] So, it appears that here we have a riot that involved manipulation for politico-religious reasons.

Politics and manipulation are often used to explain inter-religious crises in Nigeria. This explanation allows Muslims to blame other Muslims without blaming Islam. For example, the Oyo State branch of the Progressive Muslims Association of Nigeria accused "some self-appointed Muslim leaders" of creating a crisis between Christians and Muslims in the state. In condemning attacks on Christians, it explained that some Muslims were manipulating religion for political purposes. The group also condemned some Christian organisations for inflammatory statements. Christians and Muslims, the group advised, must co-exist peacefully. "Religious fanatics" amongst school principals should be replaced with more "liberal-minded ones."[62]

Abdulkadir Balarabe Musa, the deposed civilian governor of Kaduna State, in his preface to Danbazau's *Politics and Religion in*

Nigeria, recommends this book because "it traces the way manipulation of religion for gaining political power" has taken root in Nigeria. He talks of "fraudulent misuse of religion for political advantage." An exploiting class is using religion "to gain political power" as well as to accumulate wealth. CAN, according to this former governor, is guilty of fomenting "religious politics." It is not out to protect Christians so much as the vested interest of its leaders. "Everybody knows," he asserts. They exploit ordinary Christians by exacting from them great fortunes supposedly to be used for "religious purposes," but actually used for their mansions and expensive cars.

According to Musa, Muslim organisations like JNI are no different. They have "used the sharia controversy" to protect their own vested interests. Traditional rulers especially are accused of "hiding behind Islam" to further their own interests, and they do so with the cooperation of the military, police, courts, and everyone else. It has become so bad that Muslims prefer the common court system to the Muslim courts, for the latter have become too corrupt.[63]

In his foreword to the same book, Mudi Sipikin recommends Danbazau's book because it exposes "how these drummer boys of the Europeans hide behind the cover of religion to exploit the people..., and to foment violent conflicts, in order to prevent the people from understanding their hypocrisy, misdeeds and crimes."

This exposé, he adds, is particularly valuable, because the writer saw it all with his own eyes.[64]

Danbazau and the authors of his Foreword and Preface were all members of Northern Elements Progressive Union (NEPU), a largely Muslim political party in opposition to mainstream northern Muslim feudal politics. It fiercely opposed exploitation and oppression, and identified it freely among both Muslims and Christians. The party placed the entire package of manipulation, exploitation, and oppression in the wider context of Nigerian history since colonial times and even of international politics. It viewed the relationship between the West and Nigeria in the classic Marxist perspective of metropole versus periphery. Danbazau's book must be understood in that context.

According to Danbazau, manipulation of religion for political and/or economic reasons preceded the riots that are the object of this study series. Behind it all are Western imperialist designs to break up Nigeria, or at least, to weaken it, so they could access its mineral wealth. In the process they used and manipulated various agents as well as weaknesses, as they pursued their policy of divide and conquer. The weaknesses were the ethnic, religious, and political divisions of the country that were exploited on their behalf by the Nigerian "hunting dogs" of the imperialists.

Prior to independence, the Northern Peoples' Congress (NPC), the large party representing traditional Muslim feudal interests, supported by the colonialists, had already threatened to break up the country. They did this by various means, including the sponsorship of violence. In the early 1950s the NPC sponsored a terrorist youth group by the name *Jam'iyyar Mahaukata* or "Brigade of the Insane." During the 1970s, Muslim *mallams* or teachers "used Islam to campaign for their patrons seeking political office and who...were holding the reins of power." They "insinuated that anybody who did not support the party of their patrons [the NPC] has abandoned" Islam. At that time, only Muslims used this ploy.

Subsequently, Christians began similar tactics through CAN. They "openly plunged headlong into politics, ostensibly to protect Christianity and fight for the rights of Christians who, CAN leaders claimed, are being dominated by Muslims, particularly the Hausa-Fulani."

Danbazau now realized that a "new era of political rivalries using religious sentiments had arrived." "Bitter verbal exchanges" between leaders of the two religions ensued. One Muslim mallam asserted that a Muslim must become the next president.[65] A Christian leader "promptly replied that Nigeria would burn should such an event happen." The development of such a spirit was encouraged even though in the past the religion of the President had not been an issue, with Christians supporting Muslim leaders and vice versa. The "myopia" of these religious leaders has led to the riots we described in Monograph One, "ostensibly because of religious differences."

Danbazau was puzzled by the Christian invitation to evangelist Reinhard Bonnke to preach in Kano. What did they think to gain? It is well known that Christian missions have minimal effect in traditional Muslim communities the world over. He wondered why they brought in this evangelist when there was no chance of gaining converts.[66] Christians embarked on a vigorous advertising campaign with posters plastered everywhere that used the provocative language of crusade. It is difficult to believe, wrote Danbazau, that CAN did all this unaware that "there are ambitious politicians of both religions who, in a period of elections, would capitalise on it to ignite violent disturbances for their own selfish ends." So, many people were asking, what exactly is CAN after? Danbazau thought he knew the answer.[67]

During the reign of President Shagari, the Muslim civilian president from 1978-1983, a new form of manipulation allegedly took place. Several Muslim-dominated northern states voted opposition parties into power. The federal government of Shagari promptly started manipulating various elements in those states to weaken their governments. These governments and their people were put under heavy pressure and discriminated against in the delivery of development projects. Among the casualties was Musa Balarabe, the Muslim NEPU Governor of Kaduna, who was impeached.

Danbazau then goes on to accuse the Shagari federal government of encouraging the Maitatsine uprisings. These occurred in northern states that he describes as "predominantly Muslim," that were ruled by parties in opposition to the federal government.[68] He is accusing the federal government of manipulating the Maitatsine situation to achieve its own political ends, without the latter having any idea of how they were being used.

It is interesting that General Buhari, who overthrew Shagari's civilian regime and re-established the military regime, more than two decades later asked Balarabe for forgiveness for his part in the political shenanigans of that day. He wrote to Balarabe, "Your impeachment in June, 1981, might be a product of conspiracy, but you will agree that it was done in accordance with the constitution."[69] This was, in other words, an admission that following the letter of the law does not prevent conspiracy and manipulation. These can be practiced even within the legal system.

Religious crises, as Monograph One has amply demonstrated, increased in intensity. One reason was "the petrol poured on the issue by a few agents of imperialism in the guise of Christian leaders, who claim to fight for the rights of Christians ostensibly threatened by Muslims." This was made worse by Muslims with powerful connections in government who kept "calling on their followers to come out and fight Christians in the political arena." It led to an aborted coup by the Christian Major Orkar and his call for excising five northern Muslim states from Nigeria. Danbazau suspects that "some Christian preachers may not altogether be innocent, when viewed from the speech of the...Major, and the preachers' sermons in Jos about a week before the coup attempt."

Though there is much in Danbazau's argumentation that I consider right on,[70] there are parts that I dispute. For one, there is his repeated insistence that the West wants to break up Nigeria. But it was imperial interests that created Nigeria by bundling a group of some 400 ethnic groups, ancient nations small and fairly large, within one set of external borders. Nigeria is an imperial creation! The West may want to exploit, manipulate, and control Nigeria, but I see no evidence that it wants to break up the country. It was the Muslim NPC who first threatened to dismantle it. Orkar may well have learnt his lesson from them.

Secondly, Danbazau's allegation that the Church and its missionaries, through "the Pope and other Christian notables," left no stone unturned to dismantle the country during the civil war, needs to be proven.[71] I know the Roman Catholic Church sent food and other emergency supplies into Biafra. After all, it had many adherents there. It would be unthinkable for it to just watch its people starve. Allegations that the church had sent weapons and supported the Biafran drive for independence need more than general statements to be credible. Though not a Roman Catholic, I was a missionary in Nigeria at the time and published an article in a Canadian magazine defending the integrity of Nigeria. Until proven otherwise, I regard the Vatican innocent—of this one!

Yusufu Bala Usman, introduced at the beginning of this section, belonged to the same NEPU crowd as did Danbazau. Though a descendant of a prominent traditional northern Muslim clan, he published much against feudalism and oppression. Sometimes he would sound like a Marxist, and could not be understood without reference to that philosophy. Like Danbazau, he espoused the Marxist scheme of metropole versus periphery. That led him to see Western imperialists behind every tree. Note well, that this and other references to Marxist notions do not mean I reject all of Usman's views or explanations. Many of them were right on. My main problem is that his Marxism tended to make him doctrinaire, ideological; it sometimes led to exaggeration.

Usman asked in the opening salvo of a lecture to students, "Why presume that religion is being manipulated in Nigeria today? What is the evidence? Is it actually a pattern of manipulation that is unfolding? Or is it merely one of contestation between various religious faiths?"

There are those who view the upheavals as a "healthy development of people becoming more conscious of their religion, as a way of life, and rejecting secularism. Others would say...that 'these

Christians' are being put in their place or that 'these Muslims' are now being dealt with properly...."

He lamented that "there is a significant number of influential people...who deny that religion is being manipulated to serve particular vested interests in Nigeria today." To Usman, who came out of the very centre of Muslim power, manipulation was obvious and pervasive, both nationally and globally.[72]

The manipulation of religion in Nigeria is the work of the "intermediary bourgeoisie," a class created "to serve as the link and intermediary between the people and the wealthy of Nigeria and the world capitalist system. It is created to serve as the leading agent of the trading post which has been and still is Nigeria."

The main economic characteristic of this trading post is that it exports raw materials and imports manufactured goods and services without producing anything.

Usman described the position of these gate men in a rather humorous way:

> *Can this sort of person come out and frankly ask the people to follow him for what he is? So that he can take a piece of paper from one bank to another; from one factory to another, and make millions? What I mean is that the...bourgeois will cease to exist once the people can see clearly what his true nature is. Can anybody come out and say "Vote for me so that I can get contracts and build foreign bank accounts and houses with my foreign partners?" or "Follow me and listen to me so that I can get a plot at Ikoyi, and get a directorship and shares in UAC or Leventis?" or "Follow me so that I can get a big job and you can derive the satisfaction that, although you do not have one square meal a day and your daughter is deformed by and dying of chronic malaria, I am eating dinner costing fifteen naira at Federal Palace Suites Hotel on your behalf and that of others in our tribe and religion?" Can anybody come out and say that?*

> *No! That is why this class has to obscure its trust role and function in our political economy. You cannot...win elections...on the platform that you want to own houses in Ikoyi or London.*
>
> *The bourgeois cannot appear as he really is.... He has to find a cover. He cannot claim political leadership openly on the grounds that he is, or wants to be, an exporter-importer, a contractor, commission agent, shareholder, rentier, or rich bureaucrat. He has to take cover as a Muslim or Christian. He has to take cover as an Ibo, Hausa, Idoma or Efik. He has to take on disguises. He has to posture as a "majority" or a "minority." The manipulation of religion in Nigeria...is essentially a means of creating the context for this fancy-dress ball, for this charade of disguises. This game of masks!*
>
> *The real basis of the manipulation of religion in Nigeria today is the need to obscure from the people of Nigeria a fundamental aspect of our reality: that is the domination of our political economy by a class of intermediaries who are being increasingly exposed. And this is to enable this class to cover themselves with religious and ethnic disguises in order to further entrench division among our people, slow down their awakening, at any cost, even the unity of our country....*

Usman warned his students that when they describe their campus clashes as "religious," they are also victims of manipulation. "You are doing what every cheap imperialistic huckster has done and is still doing—using religion to confuse and destabilise." He reminded them that when Murtala Muhammed, the military Head of State who toppled Gowon, announced that he was going to investigate the overseas assets of all governors and federal commissioners, including those of their associates, he was assassinated within ten days! This was an economic war over vested interests in which religion was used as a tool. Having seen the Nigerian elite operate, I largely concur with Usman's description of their role.[73] Whether this is the *complete* explanation for the prevalence of religious violence is another question. Here the factors of ideology and its resultant selectivity and exaggeration appear to be playing a role as well.

President Babangida's explanation of the Kafanchan riots followed the manipulation model. Rejecting the religious motive, he declared them "carefully planned and masterminded by evil men with sinister motives, who saw the incident in Kafanchan as an opportunity to subvert the Government and the nation." He called it a "civilian equivalent of an attempted coup."[74] Nigeria, he declared, cannot afford to "allow a group of ambitious and mindless power seekers to push us into yet another civil war."[75]

None of these interpreters were original. A decade earlier there was an interesting figure in northern Nigerian politics by the name of Gambo Sawaba, the first northern female Muslim politician of note. She denied that the vandalism in Zaria during the 1987 riots was perpetrated for religious reasons. She claimed,

> *They are members of the Mafia who wish to hide behind the curtain of religion to pull down Babangida's government. You don't know that Babangida comes from the Northern Minority, and to these political opportunists here, anybody who does not come from Sokoto, Kano, Bauchi or Borno does not qualify to lead the country. They believe that this country is their personal property and once someone else is at the head, they cause trouble for him.*[76]

Such words, coming from a Muslim northern politician who can be regarded as possessing much inside information, cannot be ignored. It is the language associated with the late Aminu Kano, one of the fathers of Nigerian politics and the founder of NEPU, the party to which Danbazau, Yusufu Bala Usman, and Balarabe Musa belonged. They all speak the same language. Sawaba was really describing a climate of lawlessness where people do what they want under whatever cloak they find useful.

This climate was adduced as the real cause of the riotous atmosphere by Abubakar Balarabe Musa. Commenting on the issue of justice in connection with the 1992 Zangon-Kataf Tribunal, he dismissed the notion of justice altogether. "What justice? You cannot talk of justice where there is no law and order in Nigeria. Anytime anyone feels he can do anything and get away with it, they will do it. And in Nigeria, they will get away." He continued, "There is no law, and therefore, no justice. To me, the Zangon-Kataf crisis was not special or peculiar. Communal and religious riots are happening all over Nigeria. That is due to lawlessness."[77]

These lawless manipulators are often aided in their mission by hoodlums, young people and even children, especially the *almajirai*. Sometimes these "assistants" just join the fray to have a chance to loot and kill. At other times, they were encouraged by their elders and sometimes actually hired for this purpose. In Volume One we have seen their involvement repeatedly. In the wake of the Kaduna 2000 riots, tensions ran high also in Niger state. Rumours had it that Muslim youth were about to attack Christians. Governor Kure himself had to go around, assuring Christians that the "hoodlums" who were hoping to "to reap from the likely confusion...would be dealt with." It has long been one of the classic versions popular with governments, and continues to be so[78]—but not only of governments.

Even a Muslim leader of the caliber of Lateef Adegbite resorts to this explanation. While pleading with Muslim youths to restrict themselves to peaceful demonstrations, he felt that "it was unfortunate that miscreants often cash in on such peaceful demonstrations to embark on the killing of people and the destruction of property, saying 'true Muslims would never partake in or condone such nefarious acts.' "[80] Though the involvement of "miscreants" is not disputable, to free "true Muslims" from all "such nefarious acts" does not have the ring of truth, as the video clipping about El-Zakzaky clearly demonstrates.

A renowned Islamic scholar, Sheikh Dahiru Bauchi, condemned the action of Muslims who attacked and killed Christians that knew nothing about a certain blasphemous publication that provided the spark for the Miss World ruckus in 2002.[80] These perpetrators, he asserted, "should be regarded as transgressors." Alternatively, "Muslims should have sued [the newspaper] and the writer of the article rather than attack innocent Christians. Those who carried out that attack at this period of Ramadan cannot be regarded as true Muslims," he stressed.[81] He did not identify the perpetrators more specifically, but Islam is absolved, a gimmick we keep coming across. It would appear that he regarded them either as renegade politicians or as hoodlums, a difference not all that great! A ruckus in Lagos between Hausa and Oodua Peoples' Congress led to some 20 deaths, a lot of seriously wounded people, and burnt houses. Bola Tinubu, the Muslim state governor, blamed it on hoodlums, holding neither party responsible.[82]

Dan Isaacs, in the shadow of the Miss World episode, reported that many Muslims "are frustrated with the failure of government to play a part in reducing tensions between the Christian and Muslim communities." One Nafiu Baba Ahmed of Kaduna, felt that "as long as we have this crop of leadership, who see things from a myopic point of view, from a one-track minded angle," no relief will come. "It is political," he charged.

It gets more complicated as we go. There is also the involvement of foreigners from other West African countries that get involved in the various fracas. A number of people from the Niger Republic were caught participating in Kaduna 2000 and arrested, with one being killed by soldiers.[83] Reports had it that "some bandits, allegedly from Chad and Niger Republic" invaded Plateau State and attacked the village of Fajul.[84]

THE ECONOMIC FACTOR

We have seen that Bilkisu Yusuf has offered a variety of causes. However, for her the real cause of the Zangon-Kataf episode lies in the poverty of the area. There is an "army of unemployed Kataf and Hausa youth roaming around in frustration." That has long been a "ticking time bomb" that finally exploded. Beside this problem, those of tribe and religion play an insignificant role. The theme is a common one, going way back to the Maitatsine riot. I will restrict myself to a few statements on this theme from the more recent scene.

There is a general recognition that poverty has made people eager for change at almost any price. It has contributed to the volatile climate, for it has made the people open to anyone promising almost any improvement, anyhow. Minister of Women's Affairs and Youth Development, Aisha Isma'il, declared that it is the poor and oppressed who are clamouring for change, because they are tired of exploitation.[85] In response to the Kaduna 2000 mayhem, the Speaker of the Federal House of Representatives, Ghali U. Na'Aba, traced much of it "to the prevailing poverty in the country."[86]

This is a refrain one keeps hearing in the riot literature. It really underlies some of the previously described causes. Manipulation, for example, is clearly possible only when there are enough people desperate for radical change. Hence I do not feel it necessary to spend more time and space on the subject.

THE JEALOUSY FACTOR

The "jealousy factor" has reference to the oft-stated observation that when Hausa-Fulani people move into an area, they are often welcomed by the local people, but in due time they become more wealthy than the local people. This process sets into motion the development of jealousy in the hearts of the host people. We read earlier about the Bachama versus Hausa-Fulani conflict. The Hausa-Fulani claimed that jealousy had set in amongst the Bachama when they noticed that it did not take long for these strangers to become more prosperous than the locals. It was this jealousy that set in motion the increasing friction between the two groups.[87]

With reference to the Zangon-Kataf episode, Lawal Yusufu Muhammad represented the sentiment well in his letter to the editor of *Citizen* magazine. He wrote,

> *The bitter truth is that so long as people spend the whole of their time at "Burkutu joints,"[88] rather than engaging in productive ventures, so long will they continue to be backward. They should therefore change their profligate and indolent lifestyle and stop accusing others of dominating their economy.*[89]

In the same issue, Bilkisu Yusuf referred to and rejected the "so-called Hausa-Fulani domination" as "misdirected envy of the Kataf at the success of a more industrious people."[90] Earlier, during her days in Kano, she referred to the jealousy factor also with respect to Kafanchan. The Hausa migrants, she explained,

> *are more successful and the indigenes are marginalised. They feel their powers are being usurped economically, politically, and otherwise. With that, there is bound to be some tribal rivalry and jealousy. What we need now is some incitement through religious preaching and, before you know it, there is a riot.*[91]

Danazumi Musa referred to certain economic factors in the second round of the Bauchi riots in addition to the political. Though the Sayawa are good farmers, he averred, they are not enterprising like the Hausa-Fulani, who inherited considerable wealth from their pre-*jihad* ancestors. Somehow, the indigenes were hoping to improve their lot by destroying the economy of their neighbours.[92] Though Musa calls this an economic factor, I prefer to call it simply jealousy.

That this jealousy has served as a powerful engine in these developments can hardly be denied.[93]

▲ Summary

This final section of the chapter summarizes the major points of Muslim interpretations of these riots. The overall attitude is one of deep anger and indignation that expresses itself in various ways:

- Anger at the long history of crusades and colonialism. Current developments are seen as an extension of these historical movements.
- Anger at and deep hatred for secularism, which is identified as a Christian imposition. It is the devil's tool to undermine Islam.
- Anger at an alleged joint conspiracy of Christians and government against Islam. They are partners in crime. Government security agencies refuse to safeguard the Muslim community, for they favour Christians. Together they oppress Islam.
- Anger at everyone's intolerance of Islam, while Islam is the personification of tolerance.

In addition to anger, the Muslim attitude is characterized by the following:

- General insistence on Muslim innocence in these events. Everyone else is guilty. It is my conviction that this attitude is due to an inadequate sense of sin in Islam. Islam does not know the depth of the Christian cry of confession, "*Mea culpa!*" While Christians have long ago apologized for and expressed repentance over the crusades and colonialism and taken the church and their own countries to task, I have yet to be informed of any Muslim apology for similar atrocities in their history. Given the circumstances as understood by them as a people pushed to the wall, Muslims defend their participation in these Nigeria riots as understandable and legitimate.

- Those who resort to politics and manipulation as the explanation for riots do have room for blaming fellow Muslims. However, these Muslims are then portrayed as misguided or pushed to the wall. Islam itself cannot be blamed for these events.
- Total lack of any attempt to understand the non-Muslim point of view or to exercise some empathy with respect to them.
- Ambivalence about the relationship between Islam and politics. While the classic position is that Islam and politics are one and the same, when it is advantageous to them, Muslims will seek to separate them. The attempt at separation does not seem real or genuine. It looks more like a ploy to free Islam from its own unpleasant and unpopular consequences.

In conclusion, there is the issue about the stance of the more moderate and representative Muslims in Nigeria. If they clearly distanced themselves from these riots and clearly condemned them, one might dismiss these events as mere expressions of Fundamentalist extremism. However, apart from some mumbling about generalities, political manipulation and hoodlums, no clear statement of rejection has been forthcoming. We meet here the same silence about these Nigerian riots as people have noticed with respect to 9/11—a disturbing silence that carries an ominous aura of conspiracy. Of course, there are occasional expressions of disapproval, but these are often attempts to exonerate Islam from the onus of violence. One gets the impression that "moderate" Muslims are secretly grateful for the dirty work their Fundamentalist co-religionists do for them. They would not easily be provoked to do these things themselves, for such rioting seems barbaric and uncultured. Nevertheless, it appears to me that they are happy someone is doing it. They may even fund these activities. As they see it, their purposes are achieved without the blame falling on either them or their religion. The Fundamentalists are the running dogs of the "moderates" and serve their purposes admirably.

This thesis, it will be seen in the next volume, was firmly supported by ex-Muslim Ambassador Tanko Yusuf. Without this thesis, the Muslim picture in Nigeria makes little sense to me.

Can the same be said about 9/11? It's a question ordinary people frequently ask—and sometimes answer in the affirmative.[94]

▲ NOTES

[1] *Citizen,* 15 June/92, pp. 5-6.

[2] B. Yusuf, 15 June/92.

[3] Note how the speaker characterizes Nigeria's riotous history as "sharia crises."

[4] A. Adegbite, "*The Constitutional...,*" pp. 4, 14.

[5] L. Omokhodion, "*We Must Enlighten....*" It must not be forgotten that Gumi and many other Muslims quoted in these studies are not always fluent in English. Hence their utterances, often off the cuff, may not always sound as intelligent or reasonable as you might expect from such leaders. They are expected to express themselves in English for the benefit of English speakers who may have learned no other language. Were they to express themselves in Hausa or Arabic, they would sound much more authoritative and reasonable. So, do not let the "creative" English put you off.

[6] A. Orire, "*Sharia....*" p. 1.

[7] *Second International,* pp. 5, 10, 13.

[8] "Emir Prevents Mayhem in Zaria." *New Nigerian*, 25 Feb/00, p. 1.

[9] The initial draft of this material was written at a time of many scandals in America's business world. However, people recognize that these scandals do not represent the core of business and hence they do not call for the abolition of business in general. Nor have I heard calls for the abolition of government for its corruption. While that distinction is applied in most sectors, for some strange reason, many fail to apply it to religion and consider its distortions to represent its core.

[10] M. Kukah, 1993, p. 190

[11] 6 Apr/87, p. 3.

[12] A. Akpata, "*Stamping out....*" p. 17.

[13] *New Nigerian*, 12 July/2001, p. 2.

[14] Director, "*The Hausa-Fulani....*"

[15] *Democrat,* 19 Apr/94. It may be useful to realize that the *Democrat* is generally regarded as a Muslim newspaper. See also *NS,* 26 Apr/94.

[16] Warnings against confusing politics and religion on the part of

Muslims puzzle me, since Muslims insist repeatedly that the two cannot be separated in Islam. Are such statements perhaps indicative of denominational differences between various Muslim groups? I rather suspect it is a ploy used to defend Islam, but not to be taken seriously in other contexts where their unity is more commonly emphasized. It is a device of convenience taken over from secularism. Such public statements can seldom be taken at face value; one must read between the lines. I can do that with Christian statements, but I am more hesitant with Muslim ones. Christians, of course, mostly identify Islam and the Hausa people. To their mind, anything the Hausa do is by definition a Muslim act. Under more normal conditions Muslims would do the same. It is curious, though, that in the context of evangelism, Christians emphasize that there are many non-Muslims among the Hausa. The reason for that curious contradiction is that the non-Muslim Hausa, called Maguzawa, are not among the movers and shakers and, until recently, have not been involved in the Christian versus Muslim struggles.

17 *NS*, 26 Apr/94.

18 *New Nigerian*, 4 Mar/00, pp. 1, 2.

19 *New Nigerian*, 2 Mar/00, p. 15.

20 "Calling General Abacha." *Al-Madinah*, Nov/95, p. 7.

21 *New Nigerian*, 24 Feb/00, p. 1.

22 *New Nigerian*, 25 Feb/00, pp. 1-2. Please note the ambiguous double quotation marks in the second article.

23 *New Nigerian*, 25 Feb/00, p. 2.

24 "Kaduna Riots: Islamic Scholar Blames Govt's Inaction." *New Nigerian*, 2 Mar/00, p. 15.

25 *New Nigerian*, 26 Feb/00, p. 1; 27 Feb/00, p. 1.

26 *New Nigerian*, 13 July/01, p. 1.

27 M. Riyom, "*The History of....*" pp. 2-3.

28 A. Dan-Bauchi, "*The Supremacy....*" pp. 48-54.

29 In fact, during the 1991 Bonnke riot in Kano, several hospitals, including those owned by government, were targeted (D. Babarinsa, "*Allahu Akbar....*" p. 15.)

30 O. Awowede, *TELL*, 6 Mar/00, p. 16.

[31] K. Nwezeh, 7 Feb/03.

[32] K. Maier, p. 164.

[33] U. Salihu, "*Why Do We...?*" pp. 111-112.

[34] B. Yusuf, "*Katafisation....*" *Citizen*, 15 June/92.

[35] *Newswatch*, 20 Nov/95, pp. 31-32.

[36] M. Kukah, 1993, p. 202. Quote taken from *Gaskiya Ta Fi Kwabo*, 9 Oct/67.

[37] M. Kukah, 1993, p. 202.

[38] B. Yusuf, "*Katafisation....*" In the heat of the moment, Yusuf apparently forgot that this same question was often raised in the context of apartheid. If she had realised that the application of that rhetorical question can cut both ways, she might have thought twice before applying it.

[39] M. Jega, "*The Road....*" p. 12.

[40] M. Kukah, p. 204.

[41] M. Kukah., 1993, p. 186.

[42] M. Jega, "*The Road....*" p. 12.

[43] J. Lohor, 14 Oct/02. G. Isenyo, 17 Oct/02.

[44] Lawal Y. Mohammed, *Citizen*, 15 June/92, p. 6. Remember a similar letter in the same issue from Abdullahi Pindiga quoted earlier in this chapter.

[45] *Newswatch*, 20 Nov/95, pp. 31-32.

[46] M. Jega, "*The Road....*" p. 16

[47] U. Sanda, "*Avoidable....*" Sanda's article constitutes Appendix 6 in Volume One.

[48] M. Kukah, 1993, p. 190.

[49] *New Nigerian*, 2 Mar/00, p. 15.

[50] This riot is not covered in Vol. 1, for it falls outside of our time parameters. However, it received more international attention than any other Nigerian riot due to the international nature of the spark. The dynamics and nature of the riot were no different from the previous ones. See J. Boer, *TCNN Research Bulletin*, 3 Mar/03 and *Woord en Daad*, Number 386, Vol. 43, 2003.

[51] Akhaine, *Guardian*, 25 Nov/02, 2 Dec/02.

[52] Akhaine, 6 Dec/02.

[53] Akhaine, 6 Dec/02.

[54] Kukah, 1993, pp. 195-196.

[55] Kukah, p. 196.

[56] D. Isaacs, 20 Dec/02.

[57] A. Madugba, 28 July/03. Not knowing anything about the Academy, I have no opinion on the demand for teaching Arabic. However, the claim about the use of Arabic in Nigeria is highly exaggerated, if not downright false. It is clearly part of the ongoing "census war." Having observed the imbalance earlier, I judge the complaint about appointments reasonable.

[58] *NS*, 15 Mar/94.

[59] Reading between the lines, I detect here an attempt to clear Islam from any blame.

[60] "*The Manipulation....*" pp. 11-12.

[61] O. Minchakpu, *TC* 1/95, pp. 10-14.

[62] *NS*, 25 Apr/94.

[63] A. B. Musa, "Preface," in L. Danbazau, pp. vii-ix.

[64] M. Sipikin, "Foreword," in Danbazau, p. v.

[65] The reference is most likely to Sheikh Gumi.

[66] Though Danbazau's opinion is widespread indeed, it does not hold true for northern Nigeria. One meets Christian ex-Muslims everywhere in surprising numbers. It is true that such converts are not likely to make a public show of their interest, but that says more about their fear and Muslim intolerance than about the number of such people.

[67] Danbazau, p. 43.

[68] Danbazau, pp. 25-27.

[69] Usigbe, *Vanguard*, 21 Nov/02. It was, apparently, the season to be gracious and forgiving. Buhari overthrew the civilian President Shegari and was, in turn, overthrown by Babangida. It was all Muslims versus Muslims. The Sultan of Sokoto brought all these violent Muslim parishioners together for a session of mutual reconciliation. In typical fashion, the occa-

sion was that they had a common Christian enemy, namely President Obasanjo, whom northern Muslim elite wanted to defeat at the next election (Ibe and Oyerinde, 13 Jan/03). It appears that the Christian Yakubu Gowon, the second Military Head of State and, at the time, chairman of the Board of Patrons of the Arewa Consultation Forum, started the reconciliation dynamics by reminding Buhari and Babangida that he, Gowon, had forgiven those who toppled him and that they should do the same. His rationale was that all northerners should help develop the north and promote its unity and interests (J. Lohor, 22 Aug/02). However, closure did not come till early 2004, when Buhari "announced the resolution of the rift between him and... Babangida." This time the Arewa Consultative Forum (ACF) is given the credit for healing the rift, "arguing that the unhealthy rivalry constituted an impediment to the development of the north" (A Madugba, 7 Jan/04).

[70] See my *Caught in the Middle*, pp. 116-118.

[71] The discussion on Danbazau is based on his entire monograph. I resisted the insertion of too many footnotes at this point.

[72] Pp. 11-12. All references to Usman in this section are from his "*The Manipulation....*"

[73] Pp. 21-26. Again, see my own description of these gatemen in my *Caught in the Middle*, pp. 117-119.

[74] Please remember the cartoon earlier in this chapter about this being declared a coup.

[75] M. Kukah, 1994, p. 190.

[76] R. Shawulu, p. 126. Quoted from *Newsbreed* Magazine, 10 Apr/89, p. 8.

[77] Nnanna, *TSM* 14 Feb/93, p. 8.

[78] *New Nigerian*, 27 Feb/00, p. 2. "Kaduna Crises are Political—Minister." *TD*, 22 Dec/02.

[79] *Gulloma*, 16 Nov/01.

[80] It is likely that an article dealing with this episode will feature in a later volume in this series.

[81] Akhaime, *Guardian*, 13 Dec/02.

[82] Y. Aderibigbe, *Guardian*, 5 Feb/02.

83 I. Abraham, "*Agony....*"

84 Abdulsalami, I. 24 Oct/02.

85 *New Nigerian*, 31 Jan/00, p. 1.

86 *New Nigerian*, 2 Mar/00, p. 1.

87 Dangogo. "*Kisan Gillar....*"; *Alkalami*, 15 July/88, pp. 5, 15.

88 Burkutu is an inexpensive traditional local beer.

89 L. Y. Mohammed, *Citizen*, 15 June/92, p. 6.

90 B. Yusuf, "*Katafisation....*"

91 A. Akpaka, "*Stamping out....*" p. 17.

92 See Appendix 4.

93 *Citizen*, 21 Oct/91, pp. 7, 12-18. *TELL*, 28 Oct/91, pp. 13-16. *Newswatch,* 28 Oct/91, pp. 14-18. *African Concord*, 28 Oct/91, p. 33.

94 Even today one John Nixon from Vancouver, Canada, asked, "Where is the voice of moderate Islam?" He laments that few members of the moderate Muslims "disavow in public the well-documented excesses committed almost daily in the name of their religion." Though many Muslims, according to him, privately disagree, for example, with suicide bombing in Israel, "few will say so publicly" (*Vancouver Sun,* 8 Jan/03).

▲ FOUR

KEY PERSONALITIES AND ORGANISATIONS

Chapter Two, you will recall, depicts the general Muslim attitude towards the Nigerian nation and culture. Chapter Three summarizes the various interpretations and explanations that Muslims offer for the riots described in Volume One. That chapter is organized around the various explanations. The current chapter continues the same theme, but it is organized around key personalities and organisations. Though the explanations are similar, the emphasis on personalities and organisations provides a more wholistic and personable picture than the piecemeal box-by-box approach of the previous chapter. Covering the same territory, these two chapters complement each other.

▲ Jama'atul Nasril Islam

The Jama'atul Nasril Islam (JNI) is an umbrella organisation for the Nigerian Muslim community, a Muslim equivalent to the Christian Association of Nigeria (CAN). In its submission to the Kaduna State committee on the Kafanchan riot series, it concentrated on three areas of tension that helped set the stage for these riots.

First, there is the entire history of colonialism with its strong Christian stamp. Colonialism and Christian missions are seen as two prongs of the European attack on Islam throughout the world. The post-colonial Nigerian federal and state governments are largely regarded as stooges of their former colonial master, the United Kingdom. The post-colonial Nigerian church is a thinly-veiled weapon of Western missions. Both of these agencies, governments and churches, serve the will of their European masters by trying to impose a secular order on the country. Secularism is seen as a weapon to destroy Islam by privatizing and personalizing religion, by reducing its scope in society and, in general, by trivializing it. Islam objects to all of its facets, and reacts to it much like a bull does to a red flag. Advocating secularism is hardly a way to defuse tensions in Nigeria. This issue is covered more completely in Chapter Two.

Second, JNI complained that Christians generally object to anything Muslim. If an idea comes from the Muslim community, it is by definition suspect as far as Christians are concerned. It will hardly be looked upon in terms of its own merits. If it is Muslim, it must be part of their secret plan to subdue Christians. It is very much a cold war type of mentality where every move, however legitimate in itself, creates suspicion.

I have seen this mentality operate among adherents of both religions in surprising and unhealthy ways. Christians have their Christian organisations for medical doctors, but when Muslims wanted to establish theirs, a nationally-prominent and highly-educated Christian instinctively rejected this attempt as illegitimate and interpreted it immediately as a veiled attack on Christians. So, this Muslim charge is correct—except in its one-sidedness. It ignores the fact that Muslims tend to do the same with respect to Christians.

Thirdly, JNI is offended by the alleged widespread Christian practice of discounting serious Muslims as archaic, while non-serious Muslims are regarded as progressive.[1] Thus the opinions of activist leaders are hardly worthy of serious Christian attention, except in so far as they are understood in terms of the cold war. This accusation, too, is true. One seldom hears a Christian express admiration or appreciation for a Muslim leader, while Christians tend to admire maverick Rushdie for his courage. But here, too, the charge is one-sided. Every decade or so the Anglican communion either in the United Kingdom or in the United States produces a bishop who denies some central aspect of the Christian faith, such as the resurrection. These outrageous "theologians" are then jubilantly upheld by Muslims as supportive of the latter's views and for revealing the "bankruptcy" of Christianity.

It should be noted that these points are very general and have little to do with the immediate causes of the Kafanchan riots. As we have seen earlier, they are important components of the general Nigerian Muslim attitude towards Christianity, and are the major reasons for their strong resentment. These are the background factors that, when combined with specific provocation, however flimsy, spark the riots. The fact that the JNI report restricted itself to these generalities leads me to the suspicion that they realized the Muslim instigators had no valid specific grounds for these riots, but did not want to admit it. They had to resort to more "remote causes," the popular term in the myriad of government commissions investigating these riots.

With the JNI fully supporting the Muslim side of the Kafanchan debacle, the Muslim public expected the Kaduna Government to fall in line. They assumed that the government, in Muslim hands, would naturally support the Muslim side in these riots. The "governor should have protected Muslims against the attack of non-Muslims" by using the army. Many felt that "the art of governance ought to take second place to religion." It is significant that the Kaduna Muslim governor declared himself "ashamed to associate with Muslims who perpetrated this havoc."[2] This was not only an important and rare admission of Muslim guilt on the part of a Muslim politician, but it was also a clear break from JNI's stand.

Curiously, in spite of the previous sentence, the Kaduna Government's reaction to Christian explanations for the riots[3] was basically dismissive. It rejected these explanations because they had little immediate connection with these events.

> *They were mainly issues relating to national politics and the perceived deprivation suffered by Christians in the face of what many see as the threat of Islamisation and political domination by Muslims. These issues ranged from the OIC, Sharia, Friday as a work-free day, etc.*[4]

Interestingly, these are the same remote issues that feature in the JNI documents, either implicitly or explicitly, and that both the Kaduna Government and the Donly commission supported in defence of the Muslim case.

While Christian background issues or remote causes were rejected, the recommendations of the Donli commission were strongly supportive of JNI explanations, even though they were also mostly remote causes. It recommended a work-free Friday, membership in the OIC, the application to Muslims of the total sharia, and discouraged the use of the term "secularism." None of this had anything directly to do with the Kafanchan spark either!

How could these pro-JNI recommendations have emerged when the chairperson of the commission was a Christian? For one thing, she probably did not have the clout that most chairpersons would have. Being a woman, Donli's position was challenged by Yahaya Jinadu, the commission member representing JNI. Islam does not accept leadership of men by a woman, argued Jinadu. Secondly, Donli admitted that "they could not risk the wrath of government." Supporting Muslim remote causes would apparently avoid such risk.[5]

▲ Muslim Students Society (MSS)

The MSS may not be the most authoritative among Muslim organisations in Nigeria, but it is a very prominent one that has often been associated with protests, demonstrations and, not infrequently, riots.[6]

In an anonymous document in *Radiance*, "The Maitatsine Phenomenon: A Special Report," the writer strongly disassociates the Maitatsine sect from Islam and insists that it is a non-Muslim movement.[7] Its revolution is classified as *fitnah*, a term denoting an attack on and affront to Islam. It is basically the result of difficult social and economic circumstances that have created an atmosphere ripe for violence. These circumstances are the presence of two contradictory groups in the city: a large contingent of begging *almajirai*, children attending Qur'anic schools, side by side with a small number of the wealthy who live in scandalous opulence. This circumstance has created "the right chemistry for brewing up any *fitnah* to embarrass and humiliate the Muslim communities and to vilify and suppress Islam."

The writer of the report is therefore very upset with those that blame Islam for the ruckus this movement has caused. It is not a case of an innocent mistaken-identity problem; it is a deliberate attempt by "virulent anti-Islamic forces, including the Government, to weaken the resolve of Muslims." The federal Government explained the Maiduguri Maitatsine riot as the result of a clash "between the police and Muslim religious fanatics who were preaching without a permit." Either the Government does not understand the problems in society or it "has purposefully decided to exploit it to achieve its vested interests."

The other "beneficiaries of the anti-Muslim [Maitatsine] disturbances" are the alleged alliance between—and hold on to your chair for this unlikely combination—the "Zaria Marxist clique and the Jos Christian missionary establishment."

"Their organ—the crusading *Nigeria Standard,*" a daily owned by the government of the more Christian-oriented Plateau State, declared that

> *these Islamic fundamentalist groups are sponsored and nurtured by the dominant class of reactionary Northern politicians, [and] businessmen. Their feudal cohorts use them as reserve armies against any threat to their entrenched privileged positions.*[8]

The author of the report in *Radiance* fumes at the "scandalous and infuriating" ways in which the enemies of Islam exploit the Maitatsine phenomenon. What is there in this sect that would make it Islamic? He declares that "the sponsors of the *Nigeria Standard* have failed and will, *insha Allah,* continue to fail in their efforts to blackmail Muslims." The sponsors "behind the newspaper are part of the 'curses' which have permitted the social, economic and political structures of this country and occasioned the emergence of such phenomena as the Maitatsine."

As if the above were not enough irritation, there is the way in which the name of the MSS has "been viciously dragged into the whole episode."[9] Apparently the *NS* blamed the MSS of supporting such violence. It is alleged to have written that

> *the "religious"*[10] *disturbances in Kano, more than anything else, give the clearest clue as to where the responsibility for the recent chain of violence lies. The roving bands of rioters were reported to have been led by the MSS. The MSS has a long record of violent militancy and fanatical fundamentalism which is very well known to both the security agents and the powers that be.*

The report goes on to assert that the alliance of the Marxist clique and the Christian "mafia" are trying to "obfuscate the realities" of these disturbances. Their concern is not with the disturbances so much as "about Islam itself, which they see as a threat to their nefarious designs." And now comes the clincher: "From the manner in which the Kano disturbances have been readily and eagerly attributed to the MSS by the Anti-Islamic Front, it is not unlikely that some of its constituent elements have a hand in planning and executing these uprisings" for purposes of their own. By these comments, the MSS report clearly places these riots in the broader context of the campaign of the unholy triad of colonialism, secularism, and Christianity to destroy Islam. Christians are behind the Maitatsine riots! How the "Marxist clique" relates to all this is not clear from the discussion, but that is of secondary importance for our purpose.

The MSS presented a submission to the Kano state government committee that was to investigate the causes of the riots of October, 1982.[11] The document almost immediately launches into the usual tirade against the colonial forces and their impact on culture. It then proceeds to deny that any Muslim organisation could have burnt the churches, for doing so "has no foundation in Islam and no place in Muslim tradition. Therefore such occurrences *cannot be the acitivity of any true Islamic organisation.*" The denial is based on the interesting but hardly verified assumption that Muslims and their organisations always act like proper Muslims. What of the long periods of Muslim dormancy and its oppressive regimes that are freely admitted by Muslim writers?

The MSS statement goes on to assert that the question of the riots and the "who done it" are "marginal issues which are only indicative of the more fundamental maladies which have eaten deep into the fabric of society." There is the long-time humiliation of Muslims ever since the destruction of the Sokoto caliphate by the colonialists. There is the collusion between the Christian missionaries and colonialism that has led to the average Muslim seeing "missionaries and their establishments [read: 'Nigerian churches'] as agents of colonialism, and the embodiment of the humiliation of the Muslims, the destruction of their caliphate and the obliteration of their Muslim institutions."

Though Muslims have no hatred for any other religion, they do

> *have a mass psychology which identifies some of these religious groups with their present predicament and the frustration of their hopes and aspirations. It is this mass psychology which has to be understood by anybody wishing to comprehend the Kano disturbances.*

Without justifying the arson cases in Kano, the submission insists that

> *the real culprits are not the individuals who participated in it, but those who provoked the people into taking such action. The real culprits are those who have turned a residence into a church, knowing full well the sensibilities of the people. The real culprits, undoubtedly, are those who invited a bishop from England—a symbol of the Muslims' humiliation—to lay the foundation stone of the said church.*

That humiliating colonial system led to the separation of the rulers from the people to such an extent that they developed conflicting interests. The interests of the people were no longer significant and were usually ignored. Grievances went increasingly unheard and frustration mounted. It is in such a context, the document intones, that

> *the only means open to these unfortunate Muslim fellows to maintain their mental stability is through such emotional outbursts, against any visible targets of their oppression. It should be kept in mind that we are not justifying any action which these frustrated fellows have done and will do.*

This "cumulative frustration can breed anything, be it logical or otherwise."

Another aspect of the same problem is the effect of secularism that has "removed all restraints on human behaviour" and created a climate "of a terrifying culture of lawlessness and indiscipline." A "proper understanding" of this reality is "essential to understanding the nature of these outbursts." Muslims can tolerate offenses to their persons but not, "for one moment, to their values and ideals."[12]

There are several red flags here that are familiar by now. There is the smouldering issue of resentment for the humiliation colonialism inflicted on Muslims. There is the red flag of secularism. There is the visible challenge of the churches that represent all these negative forces. That combination has given shape to "mass psychology of hatred towards Christianity" and ended up in violence. Though such behaviour has no place in Islam, the frustration with and hatred for Christianity makes re-occurrence possible. Here we have in summary fashion the entire bag of background issues that provide not only the rationale but also the justification, even if arson in principle is not approved by Islam.

Akbar Ahmed, the narrator in the film "The Last Crusade," describes himself as a moderate Muslim who prefers peace between Christians and Muslims. However, he appears to support the MSS opinion and to regard it as perfectly plausible and acceptable that Muslims rioted and destroyed the Kano Anglican church. The fact that it predated the neighbouring mosque and even the entire community by some decades was conveniently omitted, so that the new church building was portrayed as a new Christian intrusion into an established Muslim community, mosque and all. When the police came to protect the rights of the Anglicans and shot several Muslims, Muslim anger against Christians reached the point of explosion. There was not even a hint of criticism of such Muslim behaviour, nor of any recognition of the Anglicans' long-standing rights to that property. Given the general situation, it is perfectly understandable and, therefore, apparently, legitimate. The concept of responsibility for your own actions does not seem to play a role.

The MSS at Kaduna Polytechnic were up in arms against their administration, all of whom were sporting Muslim names. Five members of the MSS leadership were suspended for endangering peace on the campus. The students were disrupting various campus events that featured immorality. MSS objected that authorities gave "unlimited permission to students to indulge in any immoral and obscene activities, thereby betraying the trust reposed in them by the parents of the students to teach their children moral education along with their various courses." The administration alleged that armed MSS members disrupted a traditional dance programme. Most students seemed to oppose the administration, because it was "hostile to the Muslims" and considered them "trouble makers." Even though the administrators were mostly Muslims, the students dubbed this confrontation as "a battle between Islam and *kufr*." They threatened to continue their confrontation as long as the immorality continued. They would not tolerate women who "obscenely exhibit their naked bodies for token fees."

The above was not the only complaint of the students. There is always that rabbit of discrimination that can be pulled out of the magician's hat any time it is convenient. During the fracas, security staff had allowed some Muslims through the gates without checking their identification. They were promptly suspended. The administration, basically in Muslim hands, was immediately accused of anti-Muslim discrimination, for they did allow Christians not connected to the university at all, to attend worship services.[13] Well, of course, what else do you expect from students?

Alhaji Sheikh Abubukar Gumi

Though there have been a number of major Muslim actors on the scene, during the 1980s many journalists liked to zero in on the now late Sheikh Abubukar Gumi. Gumi is the only Nigerian recipient of the King Faisal Laureate Award, the Muslim equivalent to the Nobel Prize. Journalists associated with *TSM* magazine trace much of the heightening of tensions between Christians and Muslims to him. Gumi reportedly said that there will be no peace in Nigeria unless everyone becomes a Muslim. That is clear language, and in keeping with other public statements he has made over time. These include the threat that the country will divide into two, if the presidency is not in Muslim hands. Another is that a woman would never be president in his lifetime. "These, and other controversial statements led to perceptible tightening of position in the...Christian camp," and "an upsurge of unaccustomed militancy among Christians," reports Nnanna.

Hananiya Zakariya reported a lengthy interview with Gumi conducted by one Yakubu Muhammed in 1987. Gumi complained that Christians "stridently" criticized him for his statements about them. "They are ignorant," Gumi declared. "They have all the chance to come to me to find out why I said Christianity is nothing." Zakariya interpreted Gumi as saying that "Islam is everything...and there is nothing you do or say that has not been regulated by Islam. Politics, economics, corruption, social relations, law, just to mention any subject under the sun: Gumi has the answer and the answer is Islam." Christianity, he asserted, has "no rules, no regulations, no anything." Christians go to church on Sundays to listen to songs. That's all there is to the religion.

Gumi preferred a political system "that is rooted in...Islam." Christians and Muslims should both have their own parties. In any mixed party, Muslims would not allow a Christian to serve as leader. If Christians do not want to accept Muslim leadership, then the country should simply be split up with one section for Christians and one for Muslims. Gumi would have no truck with compromise, for then Islam would no longer be true to itself. Nigerian unity can be achieved only when non-Muslims turn to

Islam or when the other religions "become minority and they will not affect our society."

He did agree that Yakubu Gowon, a Christian, was a good leader of the country, but he would have been better if he were a Muslim. The reason for this concession may well have been Gowon's confiscation of Christian schools and hospitals, an action that greatly supported the Muslim *jihad*.

In common with Muslims in general, Gumi denied that Nigeria is a secular country. It is a "multi-religious state." It is better to involve religion in the development of the country, for without it people will not listen. He is said to have done all he could to undermine the secular status. Though he did not specifically dub the Kafanchan riot series as religious in nature, according to the report of an interview with Gumi by the Executive Editor of *This Week*, Gumi's responses definitely put it in that category. Christians are not enlightened, he lectured. When Christians were challenged about their behaviour, they should have taken their challengers to court. But, being unenlightened, they resorted to fighting instead. Christians are fighting, he explained, because "they have seen that they are losing, because Christianity is not based on anything." It is an empty religion. They have nothing serious to do. On Sundays they go to church, sing "and look at good ladies."

"Islam changes you to be a new man. But if you become a Christian, what are you going to do? Nothing. You only say if I slap you on this cheek, bring the other cheek, I slap you. Is that a teaching?" The implication here is that such an empty religion has little resistance to fighting and violence. What Christians did in Kafanchan was "very bad indeed. If my opinion is different from yours, do you start killing me. Is it good?" In such situations you talk it over, "but if you start killing, that means you are not a man but a beast."[14]

However, Gumi also recognized a political dimension. In response to the question of what the government should do to avoid such riots, his immediate response was "I want the government to be impartial. To give Muslims their rights and Christians their own rights." That is not in fact the case. Muslims in the security forces constitute only some ten to twenty per cent. The result is an anti-Muslim bias in their security work.

> *These Christian soldiers or policemen think that since some Muslims burnt a church, they must punish all Muslims. Some Muslims were sleeping on their beds and taken away.... Not just taken, but killed. Innocent people [read: Muslims] were arrested and killed...in their own rooms and houses. I know two cases—one of them... an Imam who was coming out of a mosque, and was shot and killed.*[15]

You, the reader, in order to gain some perspective on Gumi's views, will do well to refresh your memory of the Kafanchan riots by re-reading its account in Volume One.

There is more to be said about Gumi, but, in keeping with the structure of these studies, some of it is reserved for Volume Three, where you will learn what non-Muslims say about him. Of course, as will also be discussed in that volume, Gumi had a hand in marrying the daughter of the Christian leader Christopher Abashiya to a Muslim. This was apparently not the only time he was involved in such arrangements, but that story is reserved for the next volume as well.

Gumi was indeed a powerful player who constantly irked Christians. Nothing demonstrated his power and influence more than his funeral that was attended by all the leading Muslims in the nation. As a result, the government was hesitant to rein him in, a fact that led CAN to protest when the government report on the Kafanchan riots was silent about his involvement.

THE ISLAMIC MOVEMENT

I now turn to the Islamic Movement and two of its main leaders, Ibrahim El-Zakzaky, the founder, and his faithful and equally radical follower, Yakubu Yahaya. We have already met these man and their movement in Volume One. They are alleged to be leaders of Nigeria's Shi'ite Movement, though both deny it.[16]

1. El-Zakzaky

El-Zakzaky is the founding leader of the Islamic Movement. He was born from radical revivalist stock that includes ancestors involved in the Dan Fodio *jihad*.[17] Akbar Ahmed, the narrator in the video "The Last Crusade," describes him as a devout Muslim activist, whose major concern is to oppose the increasing spread of secularism and Christianity. Christians have imposed the secular system on the government, through whom they run the country. It is a system marked by corruption, oppression, and by total disobedience to Allah. Since such a state is not based on the shari'a, it has neither legitimacy nor the right to control Muslims. Muslims should have nothing to do with such a system or such a government. In fact, they should do all they can to oppose and undermine it, even if Muslims run it who do not share the Movement's vision. El-Zakzaky served two four-year prison terms for his group's defiance of the government, only to be followed by another two-year sentence.

During his days as a student of political science at ABU, he was at one time an active member of the MSS. He became dissatisfied with the narrowly religious focus of this body and its lack of both a political program and revolutionary fervor. He felt it should be "geared towards practical and revolutionary transformation of the country along the lines of Islam," and should prepare "for the inevitable clash with *Kufr*," that is, non-Muslims. In 1979, he led a split from the MSS and established a "dedicated radical group," known as the "Islamic Movement."

The first practical demonstration of the group's zeal was a violent demonstration, led by El-Zakzaky himself, against immorality and alcohol at ABU. He traveled around the country's universities, encouraging an Iran-type of revolution. The result was that student groups in various northern cities went around shouting the slogan "Islam Only!" and painted public buildings with their colours and slogans.[18]

Frequently confronted by police and other security forces, after the 1991 Kano riots, El-Zakzaky decided to establish his own paramilitary force. Though that sounds violent, his henchmen insist that the force does not have weapons.[19] The video *The Last Crusade* portrays large groups of devout young men, for hours dancing themselves into a frenzy, until some of them swoon, not unlike some Christian charismatic groups. People around them stand ready to catch them during their fall. All of this is designed to prepare them spiritually and psychologically for *jihad*, a Muslim sacrificial war or crusade against a corrupt and oppressive secular government. That is the radical and fanatic mentality that lies behind Muslim attitudes and behaviour in the anti-Christian riots, according to narrator Akbar Ahmed. They are brought to such a dangerous, fragile, and almost hypnotic level of emotional hatred and frenzy that it takes only a minor incidental spark to provoke a wholesale riot.

The video also shows how the Islamic Movement immerses children in the *jihad* culture so that it becomes their natural way of life. It portrays children being taught to shout Muslim militant revolutionary slogans, interspersed with the well-known cry, "*Allahu akbar*" ["God is great"], all the while waving angry fists in the air with their faces betraying great intensity of hatred and purpose. Being raised in such an environment with no alternative models guarantees their growing up as hatred machines for everything non-Muslim, and ready at any time to kill, maim and destroy without any second thoughts of compassion, tolerance or pluralism.

Imprisonment became part of the movement's culture. But prison or not, the struggle continues uninterrupted right into the new millennium. El-Zakzaky, his deputy, Muhammad Mahmud Turi, and some other followers were in various jails, while a game of postponements of court hearings prolonged their incarceration.

Shortly after the sudden death of Head of State Abacha, members of the Movement staged a demonstration in Kaduna in support of their demand for the "immediate and unconditional release" of El-Zakzaky and his fellow detainees. In a press release they stated that a change of head of state does not mean the end of their cause, since they are not against any individual head of state but "against a system." The end of 1998 saw El-Zakzaky strutting out of jail victoriously. Attempts to crush his movement had failed, he boasted.[21]

Actually, El-Zakzaky had more overt Muslim enemies than Christian, and these enemies ranged far and wide. They included Muslim governors, Muslim heads of state, emirs—the whole gamut. Never one to mince words, he declared emirs useless because "they will support whoever is in power. Yesterday they dealt with Abacha, today with Abubakar, and tomorrow they will deal with Obasanjo," he declared.[21] That "tomorrow" arrived more than three years ago. Though the first two were Muslim presidents and the third a Christian, to the El-Zakzakis of Nigeria there is no real difference between them. They all need to be opposed, for all of them have accepted the secular model of operation.

Even Governor Sani Yerima, the one who started the restoration of sharia, the hero of so many Muslims, is considered an enemy. Yerima said that his worst opponents are not the Christians but "Islamic radicals." Though they all share the strong desire for sharia, they are enemies because of disagreement on strategy. El-Zakzaki insists there must be a Muslim revolution before the sharia can be reinstated,[22] an opinion he repeats time and again. With such narrow scope of acceptable ideology and narrow range of satisfactory fundamentalist comrades, there are not too many left to carry the ball forward in a manner that would satisfy him.

2. Yakubu Yahaya

Then there is Yakubu Yahaya, the "Khomeini-like *mullah*," of whom we already heard, in connection with rioting in Katsina in

Volume One. If there is a question about Yahaya's connection with Shi'ites, there is no doubting his leadership under El-Zakzaky in the Islamic Movement, especially of the Katsina branch, the most active and radical of all.

Yahaya's appointment at the Arabic Teachers College in Katsina was terminated by the Katsina State Government, because of the rebellious spirit he inculcated among students. He taught them to disregard the national anthem and the flag, for they were said to dilute faith in Islam. He also encouraged them to ignore the school's program whenever it coincided with the times for Muslim prayers. In short, he taught disdain for all authority except that of Allah.

He left little to the imagination:

> *I am a Muslim. I have the injunctions of Prophet Muhammad. I have the Holy Qur'an and I am schooled in Islamic science. I am under these rules. I am following it and I am not working for anybody. I do not recognize any authority over me but the Holy Qur'an. I do not recognize the federal government. I do not recognize the state government and their laws. Whatever my religion permits me to do, I will do it without waiting for any permission or without considering whether somebody likes it or not. I will never seek anybody's permission at all.*[23] *Do not be surprised we are using our own model of justice. The federal government does not recognize the injunction of my Holy Prophet, neither the state government. So this is clean justice. They do their own and I will do my own. Everybody should stand on his own. They are Kaffirs.*

Nigeria, according to Yahaya, needs an Islamic revolution in order to "flush out this corrupt system and establish an Islamic state.... The solution is no compromise. The solution is not talking on the table but to shed out all the idol worshippers and their leaders, and all these evils. So our aim and target is to do so here...."

Yahaya repeated these notions frequently and, in keeping with this spirit, he and his people demonized the former national administration of Babangida, a Muslim, as "a government of Satan," even though Christians think of that administration as an Islamising force. He expected that any subsequent government headed by any of those aspiring to the presidency of the country would be running the same kind of satanic system. Hence he said, "We do not recognise the laws of this country because they do not conform to the laws of Allah as stated in the Holy Qur'an. This is why we want to operate outside it." No wonder that he, too, spent time in prison.

Occasionally the Islamic Movement will organize public processions called *muzahara* that are supposed to be peaceful, but often become violent. People are killed and properties destroyed. Yahaya has been involved in several riots, but he claims that he never started rioting; it was always the police. Yahaya's people, according to him, do not use weapons. The riots start

> *when the police use batons to beat defenseless protesters, with helmet, tear gas and guns, they beat innocent people, put tear gas into their eyes, seizing and damaging their properties. Ask the people of the town [Katsina]. They will tell you who is a trouble maker.*

The Katsina riot of 1991, described in Volume One, is a case in point.

M. D. Suleiman concludes that members of the Islamic Movement cannot be deterred by threats from government or police, not even by death threats. They have a strong sense of martyrdom and fear no death. During an interview with various members, all agreed that "it does not matter to us at all whether we die or survive in (the) struggle for the establishment of sharia. God will raise other believers who will continue with the struggle from where we stop." After the Christian Military Governor of Katsina State, John Madaki, pronounced the death sentence on Yahaya, members from all over the country came to congratulate the latter.

Though the sentence was not carried out, the hysterical celebration of the threat underscores the determination of the members to carry on with their struggle against all odds.

Yahaya and his aides also have their own explanation for the phenomenon of religious riots in general to share with a *TSM* reporter. Yahaya says:

> *I think other non-Muslims cause disturbances to annoy Muslims. Muslims are peaceful people. They are not after any disturbance. If you look at Kafanchan, Bauchi, Kano and others, it was because Muslims were oppressed, or were abused, or their way of worship was abused, so they have to show their anger. So when they are holding peaceful processions or call people to see what is happening, the government will come and arrest and beat them up.*

It should be noted here that the explanation for the riots as given by Yakubu Yahaya is quite contradictory to that presented in the film. Yahaya talks as if the followers of the movement are trained to act calmly and non-violently. Riots are caused by the stupid interference of the authorities who provoke the people. The film shows that in fact these followers are consciously prepared and trained for violence.

I continue with the *TSM* report. Yahaya's Aide no. 1 explains:

> *Most of the time the causes of these riots are not properly reported. Almost all the national media were unable to get the correct version of the Bauchi massacre, which was caused when a pig was slaughtered in a Muslim abattoir. They were abusing Muslims. When Muslims wanted to show they were aggrieved, government sent the police, army to beat them. In Kano, Reverend Bonnke wanted to come and abuse Islam. You know what happened in Zangon-Kataf. It is the government that is causing the crises, not the Muslims nor the Christians. The Katsina riot had nothing to do with what happened in*

> *Bauchi. The problem is not between Muslims and Christians. We are not anti-Christian. We are against the system.*

According to Aide No. 2:"The problem is that Nigerian Christians are too apprehensive. As far as we are concerned, they have nothing to fear. If government will leave us alone, we will live peacefully with all religious groups."

When the *TSM* journalist suggested that the government serves as a moderator between the various interest groups in the country, Yahaya became vehement: "Who appointed government to do that? Man or Allah? IBB (Ibrahim Babangida, former Head of State) appointed himself by coup."

When asked about his political ambitions, Yahaya responded:

> *Our aim is to establish and pursue the system of government as dictated by Allah in the Holy Qur'an and the Hadiths;*[24] *a complete system of the Sharia. There is no difference between the Islamic revolutionary act and the political act. They work hand-in-hand, so that by the time the system of Allah is established there will be no difference.*

The next question was about the role of non-Muslims in the Muslim theocracy Yahaya envisions:

> *There are many roles they will play. They have the right to vote; they have the right to select one*[25] *of them to represent them in parliament; they have the right to get a minister or commissioner. See Egypt. Even Iran. There are many Christians there. They are holding positions and belong to one parliament like the Muslims. What we want is to follow the system of Allah. Christians and people of other religions will have the right to practice their religions, but everybody will be involved in the system of Allah. In all countries where Muslims are in the majority, Christians still hold good positions.*

Could a non-Muslim be President? Yahaya responded, "Of course, the leadership goes to the majority people. Even in the democratic system, the majority carries the vote.... I think this is justice, isn't it?"[26]

What is Yahaya's "recipe for peace in Nigeria?"

""My only recommendation for peace is to establish the way of Allah." In this context, he begins to elaborate on the role of Christianity, but it is the Islamic version of Christianity, not the self-image of Christianity, that dominates his response. It has a heavy emphasis on the role of the Ten Commandments. The present legal system has done away with all religious law and replaced it with paganism and man-made laws—like the Constitution, the Penal Code and other such things. This keeps Christians from abiding with the teachings of Christ. The same thing with Muslims; they were kept away from these commandments.

Now follows a rather crucial statement about government and Christian–Muslim relations:

> *The government comes to gather people, make a constitution which is different from what is in their original religions. This will continue to cause problems, because always, Muslims will continue to pursue their religion, but some people will see it as Muslims dominating them. So, the clash will continue, out of misunderstanding from both sides—the Christians and Muslims. Because had Christians realized that they were being cheated from God's side, they would come together with Muslims and fight this system and establish the one which would take them directly to Allah through their various religions. So, if we want peace, we have to pursue Allah's will. Christians have to pursue their Ten Commandments and other laws, and Muslims their own. Christianity and Islam have the same origin. There is no clash. But if government will come and be a judge between these two.... Government*

> *did not create anyone, so how will they set up laws for Muslims and Christians? In the Islamic world, Christians and Muslims live together peacefully as one. I will cite one example. When Prophet Mohammad (SAW) had Christian visitors from Abyssinia who had come to discuss with him, he divided his mosque into two and gave them one part to pray in.*[27] *And when he came to Medina, he called the Jews there to sign a treaty to defend the land and to help each other, while everybody would be free to practice his religion according to his way. It is the same thing we want in Nigeria. Allah is the same; all human beings are the same and the scriptures have remained pure, except that some people tend to edit their own as some other Christians edit their books.*

Asked what he was doing to have dialogue with Christians and reduce the tension, Yahaya responded, "I try my best to see that Muslim brothers anywhere try to exist peacefully with Christians, to explain to them what Islam is and even discuss the Bible...."[28]

Yahaya is disdainful of human authority not only in government, but also in religious organisations. Because of the troubles caused by random Muslim preachers, the government has given the power to license Muslim preachers to JNI and the Council of Ulamas. However, Yahaya does not have a licence: "I derive my authority to preach from the Qur'an which enjoins all Muslims to call [people] to the way of Allah. I do not need any other permission from anybody," he told Suleiman.

Suleiman has found that eighty per cent of the membership of the Islamic Movement have not gone beyond primary school. In fact, most of them are products of the traditional Qur'anic schools found all over northern Nigeria. Though he does not make a big point of it, he suggests that this low level of education during a time of "socio-economic distress" could at least partially account for the appeal of the Movement. And, I personally add, it provides an otherwise powerless, despised and frustrated people with a sense of power, worth, direction, and purpose—and all of that in the context of a virile vision of Allah and His purposes for this world and the next.

▲ NOTES

[1] Kukah, 1993, p. 196.

[2] Kukah, 1993, p. 196.

[3] Christian explanations are treated in Volume Three.

[4] Kukah, 1993, pp. 191-192.

[5] Kukah, 1993, pp. 190-193.

[6] *NIPSS,* 1986, p. 29. The report alleges that Muslim Students Society has received funds from various Muslim countries and that it has been involved in a long list of "fanatical religious actions" too numerous to mention here.

[7] This disclaimer is shared by the Muslim community as a whole. U. Salihu asserted that: "Even though the Mai-tatsines have rejected the prophethood of Muhammad, and they always attacked mosques and killed Muslims, they have always been branded Muslim fanatics, extremists and fundamentalists. We reject the Mai-tatsine connection, even more than they reject our Prophet." ("*Why Do We....*" p. 111.)

[8] Unfortunately, the magazine provides no information as to its sources.

[9] The author of the report creates confusion by suddenly switching to the disturbances in Kano. Lack of documentation leads to uncertainty here and confusion.

[10] It is difficult to determine whether these apostrophes belong to the original *NS* article or are inserted by the *Radiance* writer. It makes a real difference in how the disturbances are evaluated.

[11] Muslim Students Society, "*Submission....*" pp. 41-44.

[12] For another summary of this Muslim Students Society submission, see Byang, p. 61.

[13] "Kaduna Polytechnic Suspends Muslim Students Officials." *The Pen*, 21 Apr/89, p. 1.

[14] Zakariya.

[15] L. Omokhodion, "We Must Enlighten...."

[16] Not only do both deny membership in the Shi'ite movement, but some, including Gumi, will deny that there are any Shi'ites in Nigeria, only some admirers. Still, Zakzaky does admit to being influenced by

them and he has "an immense portrait of Khomeini" on the wall of his reception room. Some of his followers forsook him for his connection to Shi'ites (Maier, 2000, pp. 168, 174, 175).

[17] K. Maier, p. 173.

[18] M. D. Suleiman, pp. 5-6. See also *Citizen*, 19 July-Aug/91 and K. Maier, p. 173.

[19] K. Maier, pp. 167-168.

[20] I. Usman, an e-mail news item from August, 1998. This Ibrahim Usman is not to be confused with the Christian with the same name from Wukari, Taraba State, whom we may meet in later volumes. K. Maier, pp. 173-176.

[21] K. Maier, p. 175.

[22] K. Maier, p. 188.

[23] In the Ojudu version of Yahaya's declaration, the latter openly admitted that he was obeying his "master, Mallam Ibrahim Zakzaki." "Nothing is done here without his consent." See also Falola, p. 199.

[24] Hadiths are an official written collection of Muslim traditions.

[25] Note the number of Christians Yahaya foresees in the parliament of a Muslim-dominated Nigeria: One!

[26] Obviously, Yahaya assumes that Muslims are in the majority in Nigeria. That is a crucial assumption for him and most Muslims, but what is the basis of this assumption? Christians dispute it with their own statistics.

[27] This is an incident Muslims repeat time and again to prove their tolerance.

[28] *TSM,* 27 Sep/92.

APPENDICES

▲ Appendix 1

"America Is Doomed"

Muhammad Sadisu[1]

America's history has always been characterised by slavery, violence, and massacres. Perpetually used have been the methods of blackmail, coercion, assassination, and invasion to dabble into the internal affairs of weaker countries...on the pretext of curbing the so-called spread of communism. In reality, America is safeguarding imperialism, because she is created by the system and can never survive without it.

Most important, it is afraid of Islam, for as it is the truth which shines in the world, Islam exposes America's weakness. It is a nation set on the course of deceit. The continuing slaughter of innocent lives in Palestine and Lebanon is America's machinations yearning these places into theatres of testing her weapons. America's raid on

Libyan cities a few years back and the now-increasing threats to draw Libya into confrontation are intended for the sole purpose of killing President Muhammar Gaddafi, because of his avowed opposition to her anti-Islamic antics. For sure, sense has deserted American leaders. In their fit of madness, they are scheming to plunge the world into total destruction of man. Are the Americans and the Jews branding themselves superhuman? In their shallow minds, nobody deserves sympathy, no matter how innocent, if he is not of their own creed. But let a single American or a Jew die while perhaps trying to execute sinister motives; the whole world would be prevented from sleep. Are these twin evils saying only they have the right to live and do as they like on this earth? Outright stupidity!

America and her associates in the West should stop deceiving themselves that their exploitation of humanity will last forever. The blood of Muslims they have spilled will not go unavenged.

America's use of terrorism to portray the legitimate demands of the Palestinians to be given back their land forcefully taken from them, is as hollow as putting water into a basket. The world knows the truth. America and its cohorts are the real terrorists. However, when Israel bombards Arab villages, killing women and children, or when America wilfully shoots down Iranian or Libyan aircraft right in their own territory, that is self-defence! What an irony!

America now disturbs the world because Libya is about to produce chemical weapons, while unashamedly, she not only produces them and backs Israel to do the same, but also these notorious countries stockpile nuclear arms, all directed against Muslims.

America has bitten more than it can chew. Her massive acquisition of armaments, scheming, and manipulation of events to suit her satanic desires will NOT save her. Muslims will resist at all cost. Basically, America has signed her death warrant.

▲ Appendix 2

Commendable: The New Initiatives in Changing the Nurses' Uniforms

Muhammad Y. Ali-Agan[2]

It is an open secret that many reasonable criticisms have been leveled against the professional nursing uniform which was imposed on us by the colonial master before and after Nigerian Independence. It was convincingly argued that a uniform which is not more than a short sleeve gown that fears to go beyond the knees, and a cap that uncovers all kinds of expensive dressed hairs, even if worn by a woman denied beauty, is erotic, provocative, suggestive, and above all makes convenient movement and sitting difficult.

Also, it is said to be a half-naked dressing, which fails to respect our cultural and religious teachings. It is a uniform, they submitted, useful only for professional or academic prostitutes in cities or higher institution campuses and/or for a woman who has lost hope of getting a husband; so that she attracts the customers or men folk because her two breasts are, perhaps, decently standing, her bottom is soft and still rolling, her thigh down to the ankle is yet to die, and her hair is at least manageable when it is dressed with all kinds of cosmetics.

Whether or not the health authorities in Kwara and Kano states were informed by the truthfulness of all these irreputable criticisms, or by the call of various Muslims and indefatigable women's organisations, or by the tireless efforts of some nurses to gain more respect for their profession by putting on a manageable decent uniform which will recognise and respect their culture and religion, or by the personal conviction of the health authorities that the old uniform ought to have a new partner in progress; the fact remains that it is not only a right step in a good direction, but a clear demonstration that all the colonial heritages must be questioned and modified to respect and recognise our indigenous culture, heritage, and religious teachings.

After all, education has been defined as the process of preserving, transmitting, transforming, or developing the culture of a given people. The word culture embraces the people's beliefs, customs, social life, learning experiences, and interactions, among others. In another language the word culture simply connotes a way of life. The educationalists therefore agreed that any education that tempts to disrespect people's culture, or attempts to impose another culture on the people in place of their cherished one, or tries to destroy a certain aspect of people's culture without substituting it with a more genuine one acceptable to the receiver; this is not only a bad education, but will have a catastrophic result to both the giver and receiver.

Obviously, most of the educated Nigerians before and after independence realised that almost all the inherited colonial culture, including educational system, are not only geared towards corruption and immoralities, but will remain a dangerous threat to the survival of various cherished culture and religions.

Thus, an educational system which was established to produce clerks, Bible interpreters, office assistants, or translators; and above all a Nigerian by birth, but British or American by intellect, began to receive serious and continuous modifications with the hope that it will at last produce Nigerian by birth and intellect. Whether the hope is yet to be achieved or not is an open secret.

Similarly, the inherited colonial common law, judicial system, political and economic administration, social life, civil servants, and military organisations, among others, are at least witnessing certain changes or modifications; even though such changes or modifications are yet to produce expected results, it gives a sign of hope to be achieved perhaps after this century.

However, the inherited colonial religious way of life which is solely Christian, or is of Christian origin and which disrespects or sometimes condemns any other religious values and cultures, continues to survive with its attitude of suppressing any other religious values different from it.

Amazingly, all the efforts of non-Christians (or to be precise, the Muslims, who invariably constituted the majority of Nigerian population) to promote their religious values, or at worst make them manifest in their own way of life, remains intricate and impossible, just because the Christian way of life, imposed on us by the colonial master, is not ready to accommodate any value or culture outside of itself.

Little wonder it is then that all the non-Christians (or Muslims in particular) justly request that uniformed institutions and professional organisations including armed forces should allow Muslim women as a matter of right to put on Islamic-designed uniforms; that Shariah-Islamic law be given Federal Appellate status, and it should cover Muslim civil cases; that the federal and state governments should as a matter of necessity hand off from financing businesses which have nothing but bad effect on mankind, such as breweries—that Muslims be given constitutional power to discipline their brethren in faith who engage in un-Islamic deeds such as prostitution, beauty contests, pool betting or games, co-mixing of men and women in disco parties, uncaring attitude of some Muslim women to Islamic dressing, to mention but a few; that co-educational system be abolished in post-primary institutions, at least in all Muslim-dominated states; that Islamic banking system be given automatic right to coexist and compete with the present one. All these, to mention but a few, are deliberately tagged as religious fanaticisms, especially by Nigerian Southern Press, who are trained only to protect Christian values and detest Islamic ones.

It is necessary now for the federal and state governments to attend to all Muslim demands which are matters of their constitutional right; rather than being deceived by various trumped-up reasons and oppressive call of those Nigerians who want us to maintain in private and public affairs the inherited colonial religious way of life, just because it satisfied their religious teachings and condemns the religious values of other Nigerian populace. It is rather good for the government to understand the language of peaceful call and see that justice is done at least in the name of peaceful coexistence and unity in Nigeria.

▲ Appendix 3

Awake: Muslim Women[3]

Jawayriyya Badamasuyi

Oh, you Muslim women!
Arise from your deep slumber,
Islam has come to liberate
you and has prescribed your mode of life.

It is out to enhance your dignity
It has given you your priority.
Why do you need to Europeanise yourselves, all that you have?

Why have you neglected your Islamic culture and upheld the
useless and shameful fashion of the West?

Why do you need to bleach yourselves white
because the colonial masters are white in colour?
Why do you need to Europeanize your head, while
Allah has created the one that best fits you?
Why do you need to Westernize your mode of
speech, eating, walking, when Islam has prescribed the way?

Why do you decide to strip yourselves naked
on the street, when Islam has enjoined you to be modest
in your dressing?

Why do you shout the slogan "Women Liberation"
when Islam has liberated you?
Why have you reduced yourselves to objects of
entertainment for men, when you are not articles
of exhibition?

Is it that you are not proud of your culture and colour?
Is it that you deem yourselves inferior to the white people?

Do you consider the white women superior to you
and subsequently worthy of being blindly copied
without question?

Is it that you are not grateful to Allah with the mode
of your creation?

Is it because abortion pill was not supported that
you shout "Women Liberation?"
While you would not have come to this world if
your mothers had aborted you?

Is it because maternity leave is not granted to
unmarried women?

Oh, you Westernized and westoxicated Muslim women,
it is high time you awaken your sleeping brain
and make use of your senses.

These men bring and change fashion every now and then,
while they remain in their coat, shirt and trouser.

Why do you accept the Western fashion dogmatically,
regardless of the price and inconvenience caused you
and which render you naked in the street?

You must realize that Islam has come to relieve you
from being buried alive.

It has liberated you from being sold as slaves,
and has saved you from being made as property
to your husband (i.e. property for inheritance).

You must realize that men are out to spoil girls,
but none of them want spoilt girls.
Observe carefully everything that comes from the
West; we start to join in their propagation.

Try to ask yourselves the following questions
before you start in the propagation of the organisation
brought by them:

What are its aims?
Who are its members?
What is the origin and what are the reasons:
Of what use and benefit is it to you?

Is this movement actually out to liberate women
or they are after her strangulation the more?
Are there actual causes for women liberation under Islam?
You must realise that in Islam, men and women are
equal in religion but different in status.
Naturally, men cannot bring up a small child as well
as women cannot head a family effectively.

Honourable women of Islam, it is your duty
to make Nigeria an honest, sane and morally upright society.

Prove to all the men that you are dignified creatures of Allah.
Sit to your work and produce a sane society.
Nigeria's destiny is in the hand of Allah
and Allah has entrusted it to you women.
If you decide to direct her properly today,
you are in control, because you build the builders of the society.

Oh! Muslim women,
appreciate the favour of Allah on you.
And lose not your honour.
Retain your dignity.
Guide strictly your respect and modesty.

And remember the Holy Qur'an, *sura* 11, verse 138 says:
"Ours is the colour of God; who can be better than God in colouring?
And it is He alone we worship."

If you are a Muslim and believe in the Holy Qur'an
And you believe the above verse of the Qur'an, then
I see no reason why you will not hold strictly your
culture, colour, chastity and honour, instead of
holding another culture other than Islam.

May Allah guide us to the right path and cause us
not to deviate after, and disgrace us not on
the Day of Resurrection. (Ameen)

▲ APPENDIX 4

RIKICIN KAFANCHAN

Ibrahim Isa Malunfashi[4]

Unguwannin da akai sharrin,
Zan zana don a kiyaye su.
Unguwar Mai Gwado ce farkon,
In da suka dandana kudarsu.
Sojoji tare da Ôyan sạnda,
Sun je Unguwar da makamansu.
Nan ne Yusufu Zakariyya,
Ya hadu da rashin imaninsu.

Yusufu ya sha mugun duka,
 Daga gun sojan mabiya Yesu.
Dukan la'anannun sojan nan,
 Shi ne yai mai sanadi ya rasu.
A Samaru ma wani Limami,
 Ya dandani mugun halinsu.
Duk da kasancewar ya tsufa,
 Sai da ya sha duka a gare su.
Sun bar shi nan yana ta aman jini,
 Son tsabagen cin zalinsu.
Daga nan sai wasu bayin Allah,
 A cikin Unguwar Gyallesu.
Malam Musa Bala a gida,
 Su ka harbe shi don cutarsu.
Malam Na Kuraye shi ma,
 Ya dandana fir'aunancinsu.
An same su a gidajensu,
 Don fin karfi aka harbe su.
Malam Musa da Na Kuraye,
 Wannan ranar mun yi rashinsu.
To, kun ji kadan daga cutar da,,
 Su ka yi mana don kafircinsu.
Na sa ne cutar a takaice,
 Don in nuna mana halinsu.
Bayan haka sun kama Musulmi,
 A garuruwa don sharrin su.
A Kafanchan, Zariya da Kaduna,
 Na Funtuwa ma an kama su.
Jama'ar Katsina da Kankiya,
 Su ma an kama mutanensu.
An kama Musulmi masu yawa,
 Domin sun taimaki danginsu.
Wasu an kama su masallaci,

Su na tsakiyar yin sallarsu.
Wasu an iske su gidajensu,
Su na tare da iyalinsu.
Wasu an kama su a kasuwanni,
Wasu ko a wuraren aikinsu.
Wasu an same su a kan hanya,
Wasu ko a cikin makarantunsu.
Wasu ma a wuraren kalaci,
Don fin karfi aka kama su.
Wasu an yi masu fashin kaya,
Wasu ko sun dandana kudarsu.
Wasu an kulle su gidan yari,
Bayan an gama tursasa su.
Ko rana ba su gani, sannan,
Ba sa toshe uwar hanjinsu.
Wasu an su zuwa kotu,
Domin su ba su kiran Yesu.
White yai masu shari'ar karya,
Domin kishin Musuluncin su.
White ya kulle Musulminmu,
Domin bai son addininsu.
Don sun ce "Allahu Akbar,"
Shi ne ya sa aka kulle su.
Domin sun ce "Allah daya ne,"
Shi ne kuma abin bautar su.
Kuma don sun yarda da Manzonsa,
Muhammadu, shi ne laifin su?
Amma su masu kiran Yesu,
An bar su suna sheke ayarsu.
Su yan gatan Nijeriya,
White ya ki ya hukunta su.
Da ma can tun farkon rikicin,
Yan gatan an ki a kama su.

Yan tsirarun da aka kakkama,
 Su din ma an ki tuhumar su.
Domin danginsu suna aiki,
 Shi ne ya sa aka kyale su.
Bayan kuwa sun kashe al'umma,
 Duk da haka an ki hukunta su.
Sun wa Musulmi yankan rago,
 Suk da haka sai aka kyale su.
Shin yanzu ina Reverend Bako?
 Da mabiyansa duk an bar su.
Da can mun san an kama su,
 Daga karshe sai aka kyale su.
Captain Manya da Ishaya Dare,
 An bar su suna sheka ayar su.
Yau su ne gwamnati ke kauna,
 Domin haka an ki tuhumar su.
Su ne yan gata ga hukuma,
 Domin su ne mabiya Yesu.
Shi Ibrahim El-Zak-Zaky,
 Da wasu dangi an kulle su.
White yai masu shari'ar karya,
 Domin kishin musuluncinsu.
Su an nuna masu banbanci,
 Don gwamnati ba ta kaunarsu.
In gwamnati ba ta kaunarsu,
 To, ai Allah na bayansu.
Mu dai mun san Allah daya ne,
 Shi ne Sarki Al-quddusu.
Mun san shi zai mana sakayya,
 Bisa fin karfin mabiya Yesu.
Ya Allah kai mana sakayya,
 Ka tsare mu shiga zaluncinsu.
Musulmin da aka kashe duk,

Allahu Ta'alah ya jikansu,
Su ma wadanda aka kulle,
Fatan da mu ke duk a sako su.
Su ma wadanda aka cuta,
Allahu ya bi masu hakkinsu.
Wadanda aka yi wa asara,
Allah mai da masu kayansu.
Ya Allah kai masu sakayya,
Domin kai dai ne gatansu.

▲ APPENDIX 5

THE HAUSA FULANI OWN TAFAWA BALEWA AREA[5]

Osa Director with Danazumi Musa
(An Interview)

Director: Can you...trace the history and origin of the people of Tafawa Balewa?

Musa: When you see the core people of any town in Nigeria, you can easily see who are the real owners. In Tafawa Balewa, the core inhabitants of the city are Hausa-Fulani. The name "Tafawa Balewa" is derived from the Fulani language meaning, "a big black stone"; that is a linguistic evidence. The cultural evidence is that you ask yourself who rules or ruled the town. Again you can say the Hausas, because the Kanuri are Hausas culturally. Fulanis have been ruling the town since antiquity. The Fulanis ruled the town with the title Hargo. The Hausanised Kanuris began to rule the town before the *jihad*. Then we also had the Angas, the Kanuris.... In total, after the

Fulanis ruled Tafawa Balewa for centuries, then their brothers, the Kanuris, who are also Hausa, started ruling. Besides, the council of elders in the various quarters of Tafawa Balewa are Hausas. Each quarter is headed by the head of a family.... The traditional heads of the quarters for long are Hausa. By all the evidences, no single Sayawa man ever ruled Tafawa Balewa. The first Sayawa man to arrive in Tafawa Balewa is Ishaya Baushe in 1969. The man is still alive. We challenged the Sayawa to disprove this fact.... Ishaya Baushe is the first Sayawa to purchase land in Tafawa Balewa. He bought the land from Alhaji Inusa.... Before the local government creation in 1976, we did not have more than three Sayawa men with houses in Tafawa Balewa. With the creation of local governments, the Sayawas mainly were in Bogora district. But with their Western education, you cannot compare them with the Hausa-Fulani and Jarawas. They are the minority compared to these two other tribes, but they control the civil service. They came as labourers, workers, and settled at the periphery of the town. Honestly, the Sayawas are settlers in Tafawa Balewa.

Director: From your argument, the Sayawa migrated to settle in Tafawa Balewa. So where did they come from?

Musa: They came mainly from Bogoro district in Tafawa Balewa local government. Orginally they have been there. They later migrated to Tafawa Balewa town.

Director: If the Sayawa are settlers, how come they are now more in Tafawa Balewa population-wise of about seventy per cent?

Musa: How did they get that figure? Was there any column in the 1991 population census figure with demarcation into tribes and religion? How did they know they are seventy per cent.... In terms of population, Bogoro, where the Sayawa are, is the smallest of the districts in Tafawa Balewa local government. By

1985, the whole Sayawas...were 90,000. At that time, the population of the entire Tafawa Balewa was over 300,000. Go to the statistics division in Bauchi. You will have the figures. The Sayawas are not reasonable. They are telling lies. You see a Sayawa over eighty years old[6] telling lies. Even a clergyman telling lies. I have never seen any tribe in Nigeria of this sort.

Director: You have been living with the Sayawa over a long time. At what point did you begin to notice this animosity and infighting? What do you think is responsible?

Musa: Firstly...it was political. Abubakar Tafawa Balewa won elections from there. Also Ambassador Tafawa Balewa represented the area. But in 1959, one of the political leaders, Peter Gonto, became militant. As an orator with political power, you can...mislead your people just like Hitler and Saro-Wiwa. By 1959, he led the Sayawas from Bogoro district to Tafawa Balewa town. They could not claim the town, because there was no single Sayawa then in the town. However, he said they needed a Sayawa man to be district head of Tafawa Balewa. You see, if you want to dominate and control but you lack the majority, then you have to use another means, either through violence and cheating, if you cannot win through the rational way. More so, when they have good education.

Secondly, the Sayawas are not enterprising. They are good farmers, but not enterprising. Whereas the Hausa-Fulani people, long before the *jihad,* inherited their wealth from their ancestors. Because of the wealth and enterprise of the Hausa-Fulanis, the Sayawas feel jealous. That is why they want to destroy the town and always burn the market. These are the political and economic reasons.

▲ Notes

[1] See Chapter 2, p. 22.

[2] See Chapter 2, p. 64.

[3] See Chapter 2, p. 64.

[4] See Chapter 2, p. 64. I have included this Hausa poem without translating it into English. Those who can read it will be able to feel the pull of the Muslim emotions about the Kafanchan ruckus.

[5] See Chapter 3, p. 97. It is only people rather intimately acquainted with Nigerian culture and history who can understand the arguments here. Others should be satisfied with a cursory reading.

[6] Probably reference to Baba Peter Gonto.

BIBLIOGRAPHY

Abdul-Ghaniy, Muhammad H. "Lesson from the Qur'an and Sunnah: Unity." *Al-Madinah*, Nov/95, p. 9.

Abdullahi, Labaran. "True Face of Sharia." *New Nigerian*, 20 Nov/99.

Abdullahi, Magaji G. and Lawal, A. I. *"Za'a Rushe Masallatai a Jos?" Alkalami,* 15 July/88.

Abdulsalami, Isa. "Police Arrest 15 over Attack on Plateau Community." *Guardian*, 24 Oct/02.

Abdulwaha, Kayode. "Police Arrest 2 Over Lai Mohammed." *TD*, 14 Nov/02.

Abraham, R. C. *Dictionary of the Hausa Language*. London: University of London Press, 1962.

Abubukar, Atiku, Vice President of Nigeria. "Literacy in the North: The Pitfalls." Excerpts of a speech delivered by the Vice-President, Atiku Abubakar, during the Agenda for Action Summit held in Kaduna recently. *New Nigerian*, 13 Feb/00.

Abubakar, Mukhta. "How the Imperialists Are Working Against *Hajj*." *The Pen*, 15 July/88.

Abubakar, Yusufu I. *"Hauhawar aikata laifuffuka a kasashen Musulmi—Mene ne dalili?" Gaskiya Ta Fi Kwabo*, 1 Mar/90.

Abubakre, R. D. "Islamic Nostrum for Religious Tolerance in the Polity of a Multi-Religious State: The Nigerian Experience." In Sam Babs Mala and Z. I. Oseni, eds., *Religion, Peace and Unity in Nigeria.* Proceedings of the Nigerian Association for the Study of Religions. N.d. but 1985 or later.

Adamu, Marwan M. "How Sharia Was Robbed." *New Nigerian*, 30 Dec/99.

Adegbite, Abdul-Lateef. *Human Rights in Islamic Law.* Unpublished paper presented at the International Seminar on Islamic Law Held at the Institute of Administration, Ahmadu Bello University, Zaria, April/76.

———."Sharia in the Context of Nigeria." In *The Sharia Issue: Working Papers for Dialogue.* Published by A Committee of Concerned Citizens, n.p., 2000, pp. 57-81.

———.*The Constitutional and Legal Status of Sharia in Nigeria.* Paper presented at a Special Seminar on Sharia, Organized by the Nigeria Inter-Religious Council (NIREC), Abuja, Nigeria, 21-22 June/00.

Adekunle, Adebisi. "Sharia Riots Vicious—House of Reps." *New Nigerian*, 24 Feb/00.

Adele, Wale. "Hands off Pilgrims' Airlift, FG Told." *New Nigerian*, 23 July/01.

Aderibigbe, Yinka, et al. "Government Deploys Troops to Quell Lagos Clashes." *Guardian*, 5 Feb/02.

Adewole, Adebol. "Weakening the Weaker Sex." *TELL*, 27 Dec/99, pp. 9-19.

Ado-Kurawa, Ibrahim. *Sharia and the Press in Nigeria: Islam versus Western Christian Civilization.* Kano: Kurawa Holdings Ltd., 2000. This book was discovered too late to be used for this volume, but it covers much of the same materials and is useful as a single-volume Muslim discussion of the major issues.

Ahmed, Akbar. Narrator in the video *The Last Crusade.* Date and name of publisher unknown.

Akhaine, Saxone and others. "Suspects in Kaduna Riot Face Trial Today." *Guardian*, 25 Nov/02.

———, and Dadzie. "Soldiers Arrest Sharia Scribe over Kaduna Riot." *Guardian*, 2 Dec/02.

———. "Group Pledges to Expose Sponsors of Kaduna Riots." *Guardian*, 6 Dec/02.

Akpaka, Amuzie. "Stamping out the Scourge." *This Week*, 6 Apr/87, pp. 16-23.

'Ali, Maulana M. *The Religion of Islam: A Comprehensive Discussion of the Sources, Principles and Practices of Islam*. Lahore: Ahmadiyyah Anjuman Isha'at Islam, 1950.

Ali-Agan, Muhammad Y. "Commendable: The New Initiatives in Changing the Nurses Uniforms." *The Pen*, 27 Jan/89, p. 10. Appendix 2.

Anyikwa, Levi. "Cleric Wants Alleged Killing of 20 Students Probed." *Guardian*, 1 Oct/02.

Anonymous. "Nigeria: The Third Decade of Independence." *Radiance*, a magazine published by MSS, Zaria, No. 4 (No date given), pp. 7-13

———. "Iran: Anniversary of a Revolution." *Radiance*, No. 4 (No date given), pp. 28-30.

———. "*Atiku Ya Fayyace Matsayin Gwamnati kan Hajji*." *Gaskiya Ta Fi Kwabo*, 30 May/01.

———. "Don't Withdraw from *Hajj*, FG Told." *New Nigerian*, 16 July/01.

Ansar-Ud-Deen Society of Nigeria. Communique. *National Concord*, 17 Apr/88.

Atterbury, Anson P. *Islam in Africa: Its Effects—Religious, Ethical, and Social—upon the People of the Country*. New York: Negro Universities Press, 1899 and reprinted 1969.

Awowede, Obed. "Cover Story." *TELL*, 6 Mar/00, pp. 15ff.

Babarinsa, Dare. "*Allahu Akbar! Allahu Ak-war!*" *TELL*, 28 Oct/91, pp. 12-16.

Badamasuyi, Jawayriyya. "Awake: Muslim Women." *The Pen*, 15 Apr/91, p. 7. Appendix 3.

Bangash, Zafar. "Understanding the Hypocrisy of the US—the Rogue Superpower or 'Shaytan-e Buzurg.'" *Crescent International*, 16 Apr/00.

Bello, I. I. "Hello Bush!" *The Pen*, 27 Feb/89, p. 13.

Ben-Akpen, Anietie. "Govt Pledges to Save Amina from Stoning as Miss

World Contestants arrive tomorrow." *Guardian*, 11 Nov/02.

Bobboyi, Hamid. "Secularism and Islam in Nigeria." *The Pen*, 30 Dec/88, p. 5; 13 Jan/89, p. 5.

Bodansky, Yossef. *Bin Laden: The Man Who Declared War on America*. Roseville, California: Prima Publishing, 1999.

Boer, Jan H. *Missionary Messengers of Liberation in a Colonial Context: A Case Study of the Sudan United Mission*. Amsterdam Studies in Theology, Vol. 1. Amsterdam: Rodopi, 1979.

———. *Missions: Heralds of Capitalism or Christ?* Ibadan: Daystar Press, 1984.

———. *Christianity and Islam under Colonialism in Northern Nigeria*. Jos, Nigeria: ICS, 1988

———. *Christians and Mobilization*. Jos, Nigeria: ICS, 1989.

———. *Caught in the Middle: Christians in Transnational Corporations*. Jos, Nigeria: ICS, 1992.

———. *The Prophet Moses for Today: 366 Social Biblical Meditations*. Jos, Nigeria: ICS, 1995.

———. "The Nigerian Christian–Muslim Stand-Off: Some Underlying Issues." *TCNN Research Bulletin*, Mar/00, pp. 4-23.

———. "The Nigerian Christian–Muslim Standoff: The Muslim Viewpoint." *Christian Courier*, 5 Feb/01, pp. 15-16.

———. "The Anatomy of Miss World." *Christian Courier*, 3 Mar/03, pp. 12-13.

———. "Nigerian Muslims and the Miss World Pageant." *TCNN Research Bulletin*, Mar/03, pp. 36-43. *Woord en Daad*, No. 386, Vol. 43, 2003. Companion CD-ROM, 2003.

———. www. SocialTheology. com.

———. Companion CD-ROM. This disk contains (1) the text of the entire series published so far; (2) volumes in process but not yet available to the public; (3) relatively rare Muslim and Christian documents that will not appear in the hard copy; (4) J. Boer, "Nigerian Muslims and the Miss World Pageant." *TCNN Research Bulletin*, Mar/03, pp. 36-43 along with articles on the same topic written by Nigerians; (5) articles on a variety of topics related to Muslim-Christian-secular issues, culled from an international variety of writers, some in different languages. The disk will continue to be updated and expanded as long as it sells. See <www.SocialTheology.com>.

Buhari, Muhammadu. "Full Text of Buhari Speech in Sokoto." *Weekly Trust*, 29 June/01.

Byang, Danjuma. *Shari'a in Nigeria: A Christian Perspective*. Jos, Nigeria: Challenge Publications, 1988.

Christian Courier. "Islamic Dress Codes Imposed on Christian Schoolgirls and Nurses." 17 Nov/03.

A Committee of Concerned Citizens. *The Sharia Issue: Working Papers for a Dialogue*. Published by the Committee, n.p., 2000.

Compass Direct. "British, Nigerian Christians Launch Rights Initiative." <www.compassdirect.org>, 15 Dec/03.

Dahiru, Umaru. "The Politics of Sharia." *New Nigerian*, 8 Dec/99.

Dan-Bauchi, Aliyu I. M. "The Supremacy of Light over the Power of Darkness." *Leadership in Nigeria: An Analysis.* Kaduna, Nigeria: Christian Association of Nigeria, 1987 (?), pp. 48-65.

Danbazau, Lawan. *Politics and Religion in Nigeria*. Kaduna: Vanguard Printers, 1991.

Dangogo. *"Kisan Gillar da Bachama Suka Yi wa Musulmi cikin Karamar Hukumar Numan, Jihar Gongola." Alkalami,* 15 July/88.

Daniel, Alifa. *The Guardian*, 27 July/00.

Darsh, S. M. *Muslims in Europe*. London: Ta-Ha Publishers, 1980.

Dauda, Aliyu. "The Dilemma Facing the Muslim Youths in Our Universities." *The Pen*, 1 July/88, p. 12; 15 July/88, p. 11.

Davis, Joyce M. *Between Jihad and Salaam: Profiles in Islam*. New York: St. Martin's Press, 1997.

Director, Osa. "The Hausa Fulani Own Tafawa Balewa Area." *TELL*, 8 Jan/96, p. 9.

———. *"Sharia Akbar! Sharia Ak-bomb!!" TELL*, 15 Nov/99, pp. 12-18.

Donohue, John J. and John L. Esposito (eds). *Islam in Transition*. New York: Oxford University Press, 1982.

Fulata, Abubukar H. and Maiwada, Mu'azu, on behalf of 10 lecturers at ABU. "The Gulf War and the Liberation of the 3rd World." *The Pen,*

15 Feb/93.

Funtua, Umar Adamu. "Look into Katsina State Radio and Television Stations." *Weekly Trust*, 8 Mar/03.

Gadam, Hassan A. *"Mene ne Gargajiya? Shugabanni Ku San Hakkin Allah a Kanku!" Gaskiya Ta Fi Kwabo*, 7 Oct/86.

Gaya, Sani. "Look into *Hajj* Fares, FIN Pleads." *New Nigerian*, 23 Jan/96.

Glynn, Patrick. *God the Evidence: The Reconciliation of Faith and Reason in a Postsecular World.* Rocklin, California: Prima Publishing, 1997.

Gulloma, Abdullahi. "Adegbite Alerts on Plans to Disunite Muslims." *Weekly Trust*, 16 Nov/01.

Gunter, Lorne. "Fear No Evil from Harry Potter." *Vancouver Sun*, Dec/01.

Hardawa, Mu'azu. *"Yana so a hana mata zuwa aiki tsirara." Gaskiya Ta Fi Kwabo*, 1 Mar/90.

Ibe, Paul and Oyerinde, Ahmed. "Buhari Makes Peace with Babangida." *TD*, 13 Jan/03.

Ibrahim, Ishaya. "Agony, Misery of the Mayhem." *New Nigerian*, 27 Feb/00.

Ibrahim, Saka. "Ex-PDP Chieftain Vows to Reveal 1999 'Northern Agenda.'" *TD*, 30 Dec/02.

Ihariale, Mike. "Issues in the Obasanjo/Northern Caucus Pact." <www.gamj.com/NEWS1746.htm>.

Ilelaboye, Jare. "Kuwaiti Delegation to Assist Katsina Islamic Varsity." *TD*, 22 July/02.

Isaacs, Dan. "Kaduna: Nigeria's Religious Flashpoint." *British Broadcasting Corporation News*, 20 Dec/02.

Isenyo, Godwin. "Babangida, Makarfi Support Creation of South Kaduna State." *Daily Times*, 17 Oct/02.

Isyaku, Bashir. "Sakkwato: The Rape of a Caliphate." *The Pen*, 16 Dec/88.

Jahun, Sadik D. "Shawarwari ga Hukumar 'MAMSER.'" *Gaskiya Ta Fi Kwabo*, 4 May/89.

Jalingo, Binta F. *Married to Jesus: The Moslem Who Met Christ.* Jos, Nigeria: Foundation Books, 2001.

Jalingo, Nasiru A. Yahya. "Taraba Television: Information or

Evangelism?" *Weekly Trust*, 8 Mar/03.

Jega, Mahmud. "The Road to Hell." *Citizen*, 15 June/92, pp. 11-12, 14-16.

Kani, Ahmed M. "Secularism, Nationalism and Islam." *New Nigerian*, 21 Feb/86, p. 20.

Kantiok, James B. *Muslims and Christians in Northern Nigeria: Political and Cultural Implications for Evangelism*. Unpublished doctoral dissertation, Fuller Theological Seminary, Pasadena, California, 1999.

Kraemer, Hendrik. *The Christian Message in a Non-Christian World*. 1969.

Kumo, Suleiman. "Sharia is Constitutional." *New Nigerian*, 9 Nov/99.

Kukah, Matthew H. *Religion, Politics and Power in Northern Nigeria*. Ibadan: Spectrum Books, 1993.

Ladan, Tawfiq. "Damaging the Nation's Morality." *The Pen*, 13 Jan/89.

Lohor, Josephine. "1985 Coup: Forgive and Forget, Gowon Tells IBB, Buhari." *TD*, 22 Aug/02.

———. "IBB, Na'Abba Support S/Kaduna State Agitation." *TD*, 14 Oct/02.

———. "FCE Zaria Crisis: Provost, Deputy Removed." *TD*, 15 Nov/02.

Lunt, Theodore R. W. *The Story of Islam*. Rev. ed. London: United Council for Missionary Education, 1921.

Mabdul, Muhammad A. "W.A.I.—An Islamic Viewpoint." *New Nigerian*, 18 July/86.

Mackenzie, Hilary. "'Bring Victory,' Iraqis Told." *VS*, 21 Dec/02. Taken from *Southam News*.

Madugba, Agaju. "Group Demands More Muslim Ministers, Advisers." *TD*, 28 July/03.

———. "I've Settled My Differences With IBB–Buhari." *ThisDay*, 7 Jan/04.

Maier, Karl. *This House Has Fallen: Midnight in Nigeria*. New York: Public Affairs, 2000.

Makera, Salihu I. I. *"A Inganta Hukumar Jiragen Sama ta Kasa Don Jigilar Alhazai." Gaskiya Ta Fi Kwabo*, 13 May/99.

Malumfashi, Abubukar I. *"Hijab: Yadda Aka Gurbata Shi a Kasar Hausa."*

Alkalami, 15 July/88.

Malumfashi, Ibrahim I. *"Rikicin Kafanchan." Alkalami,* 15 July/88, p. 13. Appendix 4.

Memon, Muhammad I. "*Hijab* and the Intention of Sharia." *New Nigerian,* 22 June/01.

Minchakpu, Obed B. "Potiskum: Muslim Fanatics on Rampage." *TC,* 1/95, pp. 10-14.

Mohammed, Lawal Y. "Letter to the Editor." *Citizen,* 15 June/92, p. 6.

Muhammad, Kabiru. "Sharia: Test of True Federalism." *New Nigerian,* 17 Nov/99.

Muhammad, Muhammad B. "Kare Gaskiya." *Alkalami,* 20 Jan/89.

Muslim Students Society. "Submission of the Muslim Students Society (MSS) before the Committee Set up by the Kano State Government to Investigate Causes of the October 30th Disturbances in Kano." *Radiance,* No. 4, n.d., pp. 41-44.

Nadwi, Syed A. H. A. Murad, Khurram, (ed). *Muslims in the West: The Message and Mission.* Leicester: The Islamic Foundation, 1983.

National Institute for Policy and Strategic Studies (NIPSS). *Religious Disturbances in Nigeria.* Kuru, Nigeria: NIPSS, 1986.

Naugle, David K. *World view: The History of a Concept.* Grand Rapids: Eerdmans, 2002.

Newswatch. Miscellaneous editions.

Nixon, John. "Where Is the Voice of Moderate Islam?" *Vancouver Sun,* 8 Jan/03.

Nmodu, Danlami. "Our Escape from the War-Zone." *TELL,* 6 Mar/00, pp. 18-20.

Nnanna, Ochereome. "Islamic Activism: After Gumi." *TSM,* 27 Sep/92, pp. 8-14.

———. "Yahaya Resumes Campaign for Islamic Revolution." *TSM,* 27 Sep/92, pp. 15-19.

Nwezeh, Kingsley. "US-Iraq Not Religious, Says Minister." *TD,* 7 Feb/03.

Ogbonnaya, Roland and Okon-Ekong. "British MP Pledges Support for Sacked Nurses." *ThisDay,* 2 Dec/03.

Omokhodion, Lawon and Eguabor, Ide. "We Must Enlighten the People." *This Week*, 6 Apr/97, p. 18.

Orire, Abdulkadir. *Shariah: The Misunderstood Legal System*. Being the topic of the Paper Delivered During Nigeria Inter-Religious Council Meeting Held at Abuja on 21-23/June/00.

Owuna, Usman. "Islam and Contemporary Ideologies." *Nigeria Standard*, 8 Aug/86.

Radiance. A magazine of the Muslim Students Society, Zaria. No. 4, n.d.

Rashid, Syed K. (ed). *Islamic Law in Nigeria: Application and Teaching*. Lagos: Islamic Publications Bureau, 1986.

Rimaye, Musa A. "Crying Wolf Where There Is None." *Weekly Trust*, 29 June/01.

Riyom, Mohammad D. *The History of Evangelist Mohammad Davou Riyom*. Jos, Nigeria: Self published stenciled booklet, n.d. but 1985 or later.

Sabiya, Wilson and Eze, Kenneth. *Building a Church at Government House*. Letter from Christian Association of Nigeria to Governor Isah Mohammed of Gongola State, 9 Feb/89.

Sadisu, Muhammad. "America Is Doomed." *The Pen*, 24 Feb/90, p. 3. Appendix 1.

Sakkwato, Bello A, "Sharia in Zamfara: Problems and Prospects." *New Nigerian*, 5 Jan/00.

Salihu, Ustaz S. "Why Do We Experience Fanaticism? A Muslim Perspective." See *The Second International Conference on Christian–Muslim Mutual Relations* below in this Bibliography. Pp. 109-112.

Sanda, Umar. "Avoidable Carnage in Kaduna." *New Nigerian*, 27 Feb/00.

Scott, H. S. "The Development of the Education of the African in Relation to Western Contact." *The Year Book of Education*. London: Evans Brothers, 1938.

The Second International Conference on Christian–Muslim Mutual Relations: Report and Papers of a Conference Initiated by the Lutheran Church of Christ in Nigeria and Sponsored by the Evangelical Lutheran Church in America. Held in Miango, Plateau State, Nigeria, 11-16 Sept./95.

Shaw, Flora L. *A Tropical Dependency*. London: James Nisbet, 1905.

Shomotum, Muhammad B. "*Hijab*: A Must for Muslim Women." *The Pen*, 10 Mar/89. p. 10.

Suleiman, Ibraheem/Ibrahim. *Islam, Secularism and Nigeria*. Paper delivered to the Muslim Forum, Ahmadu Bello University. March, 1986. Appendix 4 in Monograph 4.

———. *State and Religion in Nigeria: A Suggested Framework*. Commissioned paper submitted to the Political Bureau, Lagos. Zaria: Centre for Islamic Legal Studies, Ahmadu Bello University. May, 1986.

Suleiman, Mohammed D. *Islamic Fundamentalism: The Shias in Katsina*. Conference on Islam and the History of Learning in Katsina State. Katsina, 11 May/92.

Taiwo, Juliana. "Zamfara Pledges Support for Mathematical Studies." *TD*, 13 Nov/02.

Takaya, B. J. and Tynden, S. W. (eds). *The Kaduna Mafia: A Study of the Rise, Development and Consolidation of a Nigerian Power Elite*. Jos, Nigeria: University of Jos, 1987.

TEKAN. *Towards the Right Path for Nigeria*. Jos, Nigeria: TEKAN, 1987.

Tofa, Bashir O. "The Divine and the Devilish." *The Pen*, 16 Dec/88, p. 7.

Tom, Muhammad H. "Fundamental Human Rights: Evolution and Development." *New Nigerian*, 3 Jan/00, p. 20.

Umar, Ibrahim M. "Sharia Respects Pluralism—Ibrahim Suleiman." *New Nigerian*, 2 Nov/99, p. 20.

Usigbe, Leon "'Buhari Is Fascist, Doesn't Forgive,' Says Balarabe Musa in Comments over Apology Letter." *Vanguard*, 21 Nov/02.

Usman, M. T. "FG, Don't Hands off *Hajj* Operations." *New Nigerian*, 28 June/01.

Usman, Yusufu B. *For the Liberation of Africa*. London: New Beacon Books, 1979.

———. (ed). *Political Repression in Nigeria*. Kano: Bala Mohammed Memorial Committee, 1982.

———. *The Manipulation of Religion in Nigeria*. 1977-1987. Kaduna: Vanguard Printers, 1987.

Weekly Trust. Miscellaneous editions.

Yahaya, Bashir. "Sharia: The Misunderstood Concept." *New Nigerian*, 3

Dec/99.

Yusuf, Bilkisu. "'Katafisation' of Mankind." *Citizen*, 15 June/92, p. 33.

Yusuf, Razak. "51 Held, 10 Injured as Fanatics Invade Ibadan Schools." *TD*, 20 Feb/03.

Zakariya, Hananiya. "Interview with Sheikh Abubakar Mahmoud Gumi." *Quality*, 9 Oct/87, pp.34-39.

Valuable Ongoing Web Resource:

Check out <www.CompassDirect.org>, Nigeria page, for a list of relevant articles on Muslim-Christian relations. However, be aware they are written from a Christian perspective.

INDEX